Sceptered Isle
The Countryside of Britain

Sceptered Isle
The Countryside of Britain

James Turner
Photographs by Edwin Smith

Methuen · New York · Toronto

Text © The Executors of the late James Turner 1977
Photographs © Olive Smith

First published in Great Britain in 1977
by Ward Lock Limited, 116 Baker Street,
London W1M 2BB, a member of the Pentos Group.

First published in North America 1977 by
Methuen Publications, 2330 Midland Avenue,
Agincourt, Ontario. (A Division of The Carswell
Company Limited.)

Canadian Cataloguing in Publication Data

Turner, James.
    Sceptered Isle

Includes index.
ISBN 0-458-92460-1

1. Great Britain—Description and travel—1971.
2. Physical geography—Great Britain. I. Title.

DA632.T87   914.1′04′857   C77-001098-9

Printed in Italy

Previous page Tennant Gill, Fountains Fell,
Yorkshire

Contents

Publishers' Note

At the time of his death the author had completed the
final draft of the manuscript but had not prepared
a full list of acknowledgments. The publishers would
like to thank all those who helped James Turner in
the preparation of this book, whom he would certainly
have wished to acknowledge by name. They would also
like to thank Olive Smith for all her help in making
this selection from her husband's photographs and
writing the captions to them.

Introduction

Landscape is among the most potent of the influences which form and govern us. We begin, simply and involuntarily, by taking it in as part of the indigenous nourishment at hand when we enter the world, and we eventually need and accept it as a philosophy. No one is exempt from some kind of pressure which is set up by his surroundings and for many this is of the most profound personal importance. 'Those scenes made me a painter', wrote John Constable, indicating a little Suffolk–Essex valley. D. H. Lawrence too, one of the best landscape descriptive writers, felt that he was as much a creation of Nottinghamshire's scenery, Industrial Revolution streets and hilly farms alike, as of blood. And we can all say to some degree that 'those scenes', wherever we grew up, are more likely influences than anything to be found in our stars. Even the lack of landscape is formative and people who cannot see the earth for the concrete or the distance because of the development often reveal compensatory factors in their make-up.

As for the indebtedness of art to landscape, it is both inevitable and immeasurable. From music-landscapists like Delius to poets, painters, sculptors and architects of all types and all times, it is the light, textures, motifs, rhythms, shapes, colours and language of the natural world which are the source of all their metaphor and imagery. And, for the most tried, trustworthy and easily available ingredient for human happiness, what is there to beat scenery? Every great religion emphasizes the need to transcend earthiness – and symbolically teach us how to achieve this state by beguiling us with vistas of godly mountain tops, sacred streams and promising plains. Thus we reach spiritual bliss via geography. *'Un paysage quelconque est un état de l'âme'* – 'Any landscape is a condition of the spirit', wrote the Swiss author Henri-Fréderic Amiel in his private journal. His spectacular one was literally believed to be so by countless British clergymen and intellectuals who sought the Jungfrau as earnestly as we moderns have trekked to the heights of Katmandu. Now and then there has been resistance to landscape preoccupation. Keats said that 'scenery was fine, but that human nature was finer'. But he was temporarily exhausted by the cult of landscape as it was preached by Wordsworth and his followers. Also he was a London boy whose meadows and rivers had been discovered in the pages of Shakespeare and Spenser. For John Keats, via earlier poets, landscape was a sumptuous attack on the senses.

James Turner, who completed this highly individual glance at Britain during the last months of his life, was the perfect writer for keeping a view in its place.

He could leave part of himself in a scene and he never went around insisting, as so many do, that the countryside had a duty towards him. In fact, he rather liked its inhuman force. I have often watched him on the Lizard, in some Suffolk field or staring about him in Wales with a kind of relish of his own brevity in comparison with that of the vistas stretching before him. Unlike Richard Jefferies, he was actually comforted by human transience and what might be called Nature's detachment. Jefferies acknowledged yet deplored scenery's inability to love him back.

In Britain one is conscious of an intensely used landscape and, regretfully here and there, a still exploited landscape, but never a subdued landscape. Each generation is both improver and vandalizer and Time manages to make a soft mark on bad and good alike. These words and pictures do much to improve our views on the view, as it were. It is, on the whole, a confirmatory book and it makes us eager to go outside and look around, as the poet Ted Hughes suggests, at,

> *The convenience of the high trees!*
> *The air's buoyancy and the sun's ray*
> *Are of advantage to me;*
> *And the earth's face upward for my inspection.*

Whilst James Turner's feeling for the countryside was literary and reflective, as well as practical, it would never have occurred to him that it should have been aware of his existence. On the contrary, the fact that he knew it to be the main source of his imaginative power and the centre of happiness and well-being made it seem something before which he had to be thankful.

We had been close friends for just on thirty years and during this long time we wandered about in many of the places to which he returns in this book. Thus many of these tours are as evocative of my life as his. And although I never met Edwin Smith, who died shortly before James, we both tremendously admired the architectural and topographical books which he and his wife Olive Cook produced. Nothing could be better than that two such gifted commentators on rural Britain should share these final pages.

James Turner was the perfect explorer-companion on any outing. The botanizing, church-crawling, discursive forays we first made in East Anglia eventually extended themselves to the West Country and to Wales. His sprawling knowledge of the scientific and the abstruse, literary allusion and folklore, would come into play the minute we set off. He was also one of those lucky people who understood drift and leisure, silence and the virtues in just muddling about. He had a knack of making all these things work for him in parallel, so to speak, and I never met anyone who succeeded in gaining, from a purely literary point of view, such tangible returns from a day on Bodmin Moor or a drive through Conway Valley. Like most creative people, he particularly loved associative places, and he would use a planned visit to Edward FitzGerald's grave at Boulge, a Celtic shrine in south Cornwall, Baring-Gould's rectory at Lewtrenchard, a medieval pilgrim-route or the habitat of some bird or plant as the *raison d'être* for what would eventually prove to be a whole mass of ramified travel experiences which were centred upon this special spot. Our last associative-cum-everything else jaunts together were to see the setting of Thomas Hardy's early novel, *A Pair of Blue Eyes*, near Boscastle, upon which I was doing some critical work and, of course, soon we were extending this visit to the frightening geology of the nearby cliff-face and to Parson Hawker at Morwenstowe. I recall how then his landscape talk united the earth's skin and its recent history with the rock it covered.

He was a compulsive recorder – some writers, paradoxically it may seem, are not – and he turned everything that happened to him into poems, stories and essays. Landscape happened to him in a big way and all he wrote is as much dominated or controlled by place as by people. He was in the correct and necessary sense provincial; a large part of his gift was his ability to recognize all kinds of regionalism and to make the links showing them to be interrelated and forming a whole. This is very apparent here. During the last year or two of his life, James Turner went over all the old ground of his topographical experience, either in retrospect or in that adventurous little car of his in order to bring the constituents of our British scenery together in a personal way. A good deal of his book is a place-autobiography and readers who share the experience of 'being there makes you part of it' will understand the involvement. And they will certainly see themselves in his adoption of roads, canals, rivers, hills, climates, etc., as contact with their own favourite discovered features of our island produces its sense of possession.

While he was writing this delightful book, James Turner was himself beginning to discover and possess Yorkshire. Some of its little country towns had taken him by storm. He wrote to me about them. Why had he not really *seen* them before? How pleasant to live in one of them!

Ronald Blythe

The Landscape

THE enormous variety of the British countryside is what makes a journey through landscape so infinitely rewarding. From the magnificent seascapes of the west, through the downlands of Wiltshire, Kent and Sussex, to the fenlands of Lincolnshire, the change is sharp. When you leave the warmth of the south and penetrate the industrial landscapes of the Midlands, and come out on the Pennines and the Lakes, and so to the Scottish lochs, the change is sharper still.

The journey is not only a physical one, nor even an historical one (though this is valid enough). It is also a spiritual journey. Perhaps this is the most important, for to the Englishman, the Scotsman and the Welshman the landscape of his homeland is his deepest spiritual experience. He is remade within the country-side. The woods and streams still hold an undefined comfort for him; the moors, the mountains, the cruel seascapes, still hold him in awe. He may no longer believe in God; he believes emphatically in himself and in his place in nature. This is so however much he scars the Cornish and Devon moorland with china clay rubbish heaps, or Wales and the Midlands with coal slags. However much he pollutes the estuary waters round the coast with the effluent of nuclear power stations and factory-waste, he believes in the countryside as his true home.

For one man it may be the ancient oak and holly forest of Staverton Thicks in Suffolk; for another the neolithic flint mines on the Breckland heaths in Norfolk; for another the view from Kingswood Common, near Kington, in Herefordshire, or the Malvern Hills, with the valley of the Wye below, where Langland sat writing his poem *Piers Plowman* in 1362; or it may be the hop-fields of Kent, the wide ranges of the Cheviot Hills, or Dungeon Ghyll in Great Langdale, leading to the Three Tarns and the Lingcove Beck in Eskdale, or the great Welsh reservoirs and dams. But for all it is the special place of refreshment and restoration.

The evidence for this is large, as witness the growing membership of trusts such as the National Trust, Enterprise Neptune, which has saved so much of the coastline, and the Association of Nature Conservation Trusts. The fact that the Dartmoor authorities are suggesting dividing up the moor into sections, and when one part is full of summer visitors, closing it for the day and directing people to other areas; and the wearing away of such beauty spots as Kynance Cove in Cornwall, or the Pig Track up Snowdon by the feet of countless walkers is proof of man's longing for the countryside. For the 'rush to the country' is not only a desire to leave behind the concrete wilderness of

Walberswick, Suffolk
It is a day in October following a memorable storm and the breakers still heave and crash with the metallic glitter encouraged by a cold wind and angry, intermittent sunshine. The photograph captures the untamed spirit of this beach and hints at the possibility of the sea raging up the shore and surging inland. And there is indeed continual if seldom perceptible encroachment here.

The character of this coast, prone to erosion, bordered by marshes and intersected by mazy rivers, sometimes running parallel to the sea, explains why a lonely shore such as this is a common sight in Suffolk: it is impossible to follow the line of the beach with a road such as has brought unsightly development and excessive tourism to so much of the English coast.

Cotterdale, Yorkshire
We are in dale country near Hawes, in a tributary of Wensleydale, where the shape of the terraced landscape is determined by layers of pale-grey limestone, ochre-coloured sandstone and dark-grey shale. They are the material of this little farmstead and its enclosing walls. It is not at all uncommon, when walking in the Dales, which are still sparsely populated and free of industry, to be suddenly confronted by a scene of timeless green enchantment such as this.

cities; it is the slaking of a spiritual thirst, without which man could not exist. Indeed, if it is denied him, he *will* cease to exist.

The landscape, then, is immensely important. What matters is the actual feel of the earth, the feel of seeds in the hand, the touching of wild flowers, the moss on trees, the walking in woodland and open fields, the smell of a fox in a spinney, the cool sea waters, the touching of stones, say in Hadrian's Wall. All these are the clothing of landscape, the integral parts of the scenery.

Two revolutions have cut down the countryside and the landscape in this century. The first was the 1914 War, before which there had been little change over hundreds of years, except for the agricultural improvements of such men as Coke of Norfolk and 'Turnip' Townshend. And then there was the Second World War, after which the flight of men from the land reached the huge total of 20,000 a year. This was followed by the connecting of all farms to the National Electricity Grid, and the introduction of massive machines to take the place of men and horses.

The consequences of such an erosion of manpower has meant the cutting

12

down of hedges, which, as it were, framed the countryside; it has meant the building of great grain silos and the growth of factory farming. In short it is scientific farming which has radically altered the countryside, and not always for the better. Trees have been felled, rivers polluted, soil has been eroded, and millions of fir trees have been planted by the Forestry Commission to take the place of indigenous woods.

Britain is now no more than a series of pockets of landscape scored by industrialism, divided by endless, wide motorways. Some of these pockets, like the Yorkshire dales and moors, are enormous, but even they are being eroded by the War Ministry and by Early Warning Systems, in the same way that the coastline is spawning atomic power stations, with pylons and wires cutting into every foot of the old landscapes.

Yet the permanencies of landscape remain. It is vital that they be preserved. Large areas of Britain are visited by thousands in the summer. Most of these places remain inviolate in winter. A thousand years of battering seas will be needed to alter significantly the Cornish or Welsh coastline; a similar length of time materially to change the face of Snowdon. The countryside of Britain, provided it is cared for, is timeless.

Anstey, Hertfordshire
A greater contrast to the photograph of Cotterdale on the left could scarcely be imagined. Chalk here takes the place of sandstone foundations and whereas the charm of the Yorkshire scene depends on the luxuriance of trees, the appeal of this Hertfordshire landscape is that of burgeoning fields wrested from the forest. For this whole terrain was one of the most thickly wooded areas of England and the cottages are part of an irregular, straggling village created by individual settlement in woodland clearings.

1 Mountains

'MOUNTAINS', said G. K. Chesterton, 'are to be looked up at not down from.' Where total landscape is concerned he was right. The man or woman who climbs a mountain does so in order to emerge into a solitary and eclectic landscape seen only by the few.

Dr Johnson was right, too, when he called a mountain 'a considerable protuberance'. Right, at least, for England, whose highest peak is Scafell Pikes, at 3,210 feet. The grandeur of this mountain forms the geographical centre of Lakeland. Yet Johnson had also been to Wales and had 'Been upon Penmaenmawr and Snowdon' in the summer of 1774. I do not think he got very far up the mountain, for this was the eighteenth century, when 'raw' nature, as manifest in such places as the Welsh mountains, the Highlands of Scotland, or the wilder parts of Cumberland, Yorkshire and Derbyshire, was regarded with horror, only to be contemplated in the security of the library or boudoir. The preference then was for a well-ordered, pastoral landscape. There was no knowledge of the motives which impel us of the twentieth century to look for beauty in wildness, no urgent need to escape from concrete jungles or the ceaseless noise of daily work. Now, with a railway actually taking you to the top of Snowdon, even this most dramatic of mountains has become well ordered. Dr Johnson would have approved.

Brilliance of light is the outstanding characteristic of these towering ends of landscape. To stand on any of the paths leading towards Snowdon, to come to Llanberis Pass through the mountains, or to the village of Beddgelert, is to be aware of something beyond our ordinary, townscaped minds and senses. Here is a depth of vision leading you into the centre of an almost untouchable landscape, into a world of pure air and clear light above the valleys. To walk any of the well-known paths to the summit is still an adventure in a dream landscape which at any moment may become too real. Evidence of this is in the numerous rescue schools and rescue points.

Snowdon, the highest Welsh mountain, has a presence all its own. Walk the Beddgelert Track (the easiest path) and you come, after a mile, into the fastnesses of this mountain landscape. The air is completely different, exhilarating, matched by that of the Pennines and of Scotland. This is a climber's landscape. At every stop you make in the Snowdon National Park you will see them on the precipitous rock faces, such as that of Glyder Fach, or walking the roads with ropes over their shoulders and pitons rattling at their waists. They seem to belong to a different kind of race from urban man, his offices and homes,

The Snowdon range from Bewdy Newydd, Merioneth The winter light strikes the upland valley and gleams on the snowy peaks of some of the oldest formations in England and Wales. The schists, shales and slates of these Welsh ranges were deposited granule by granule through millions of years in seas where primitive soft-bodied and molluscous life-forms were only beginning to emerge. Volcanic upheavals in the sea-bed sent up mountain masses of solidified lava, more enduring than the rocks it covered or by which it was itself submerged when the land sank below the sea during the 130 million years of the Carboniferous and Cretaceous periods. For although by comparison with our own puny, transient existences the craggy beauty of the mountains seems changeless, it is no less impermanent and is being ceaselessly transmuted by the processes of attrition, denudation and disintegration.

The photograph emphasizes the contrast between the remoteness of the ancient rocks and the domesticity of the stone-built, isolated farms, and also reveals the remarkable shapeliness of the Welsh mountains, so composed that they achieve a more impressive grandeur than heights of four times their altitude.

though they will almost certainly have come from towns. It is fitting that these climbers form a 'secret society', with their own separate rooms in the pubs.

In north Wales you cannot escape Snowdon unless the summit is blanketed by cloud. One of the most perfect long-landscape views of the mountain is from the gardens of Bodnant, four miles south of Conway in Denbighshire. These gardens, begun in 1875 and now belonging to the National Trust, are an oasis of colour and ornament. Laid out in a frame of native trees, a variety of shrubs and conifers flourish in a series of beautiful and interesting gardens, from the long laburnum walk and arch to the immense water garden. From these terraces, when the light is of the exact lucidity, you feel that you can reach out and touch Snowdon in the distance. At others, the light dark and overcast, so far off does Snowdon appear that you begin to understand the power that such mountains have on the mind of man. 'To be looked up at.' Indeed!

One of the greatest virtues of the Welsh mountain farmer is his courtesy. Such farmers are different from lowland men. They have the feel of rock faces in their hands at all times. Their bodies are attuned to winds and snow and exposure. I have spent a whole afternoon talking to such a man when once I lost my way in the slate lanes about Dylife, the old lead-mining village high in the mountains above Aberdovey and the sea. This is a land of rock, heather and bog, not much changed since the Ice Age; a land of great silences, broken only by the bleat of lambs, the sharp bark of sheep dogs, or the sudden flight of snipe or grouse.

The farmer, who was cutting logs with a handsaw, had all the time in the world to tell me about the local beauty spots and wild life. Below us was the lake, Llyn Glaslyn, and to the right the high wall of the plateau. Once up there, he said, nothing obscures your view of Plynlimon and the source of the river Severn. On fine days you can go into a slate deposit above Dylife and look over to Snowdon and its sister mountains in the distance.

This mountain country is full of deserted cottages, reminders that in the old days the hill farmer and his family passed the summer in the mountains and only came down to a more substantial house – the *hendre* – for the winter. I went up to one of these *hafods* above Betws-y-coed, high above the road, tucked away into groves of sycamore, birch and elm. Small and massively built of granite, like all the Welsh cottages and farmsteads, it was approached up the side of a clear mountain stream. Above it was sweet water and birdsong.

I stood with the whinberry bushes at my feet. It was late August, and I could see across the top of the hill a farmer with his dogs at the August gathering, the bringing down of the sheep from the mountains. It might have been a picture by the nineteenth-century Kentish painter Samuel Palmer. The work of gathering falls mainly on the famous Welsh sheep dogs, who have to find the sheep before marshalling them into pens of dry stone. And with the sheep are the curlews in their flocks of thousands feeding on the damp moorlands. Their cries, at first of joy and then a long despairing lament, seem to haunt Wales eternally.

Wales, or at least north Wales, is a country composed almost entirely of palaeozoic rocks divided by deep valleys. These twisted rocks with their denuded surfaces were produced by ice pressures millions of years ago. In this great mass Snowdon, 3,560 feet high, Carnedd Llywelyn, 3,484 feet, and Carnedd Dafydd, 3,426 feet, are sister peaks. Above the 2,000-foot line these stupendous rock formations are bare. In winter they are snow covered, their summits reflected in lonely lakes high in the mountains. On the Pig Track up Snowdon these are deep blue or black and rounder in shape than the valley lakes. South and east of Snowdon, and still at about 2,000 feet, are the Harlech Dome, the Arenig moorlands and the Berwyn mountains. You come through a long rolling landscape full of deserted ruined cottages, which forms a central plateau with Plynlimon, 2,469 feet, as the dominant feature, to a region of high moorland lying in boulder clay, full of bogs in the cold wet subsoil. Before you descend into the coal-mining areas to the south, there are outstanding sandstone hills such as Radnor Forest, 2,163 feet, and the steep uprisings of the Brecon Beacons, the Black Mountains and the volcanic rocks of Breidden.

One other mountain forces its personality upon you. As you come down the Pass of Aberglaslyn to the town of Dolgellau, you can see Cader Idris before you on the left hand, with glimpses of the long lake, Tal-y-llyn, below it. Cader Idris, although it is 2,927 feet high, is a 'comfortable' mountain. That is, it does

A farmer and his wife, Ystrad Meurig, Cardiganshire
Even today the untamed mountains dominate those who pass their days among them. At the time when the photograph was taken, almost twenty years ago, this farmer and his wife lived on their 25 acres in a solitude unimaginable to city dwellers. Neither had had more than four years' schooling; but a stranger meeting them was struck by their tranquillity, their dignity and gentle courtliness. Mr Evans had worked from the age of ten, when he was employed for a wage of 1s. 6d. a week in winter and 1s. a week in summer. On his own boggy terrain he used none but traditional implements.

Descent from Cader Idris, Merioneth
Like Snowdon, Cader Idris is formed of volcanic material of immense hardness. The shattered boulders which litter the slopes, like the great cwms beneath the summit of the mountain, are relics of the Ice Ages, the last of which ended some 20,000 years ago. Although at this stage of the descent the full ferocity of the upper slopes has abated, the crags replaced by stretches of bog and whinberry, this scene with its vast indigo, cloud-misted distances, pervaded by a sweet peaty smell and echoing with the wild plaint of the curlew, is both exhilarating and intimidating in its splendid immunity from traces of human activity.

not seem unclimbable by the amateur, as does Snowdon. Even if Cader is impressive, it is still welcoming. Perhaps its personality is due to the fact that it is named after Idris, a descendant of Merion, who founded the shire of Merioneth and who was killed in battle beside the river Severn.

Mountains are the Gothic drama of landscape; their dramatis personae the rare and exciting animals and flowers to be found amongst them, such as the polecat, the mountain hare, the ptarmigan, the capercailzie and the dotterel, which lives only on the highest mountains. The mountain ringlet, the only alpine butterfly in Britain, is also found here. As for grasses there is sheep's fescue, mat grass, stiff sedge, three-leaved rush and spiderwort, which is found only in Wales.

Two years ago I planted a mountain ash in my garden in Cornwall, and at the same time broadcast the seeds of Welsh poppies, which I gathered from plants growing on rock ledges below Snowdon. The rowan tree, as the mountain ash is known, is supposed to keep off witches. Its crimson berries light the mountain lanes in autumn. The yellow poppy when it is first seen is as good as sunlight.

Among the less common plants to be found here are the golden saxifrage, which flowers in the spring, and the white starry saxifrage. The rock ledges of

the mountains provide a kind of alpine climate for many plants, and you may often come across other saxifrages such as the purple and the late flowering moss saxifrage. But most lovely of all is the yellow globe flower, which grows in the volcanic ash of Cader Idris and of Snowdon.

My own particular memory of such wild flowers is of the day when I first saw growing, by the great reservoir lakes of mid-Wales, in a meadow below an enormous upthrust of mountain, the yellow heart's ease or mountain pansy. Its mauve and yellow petals have symbolized for me ever since the mountain landscape of Wales.

If you go directly east from Snowdon, you arrive in the Peak district in Derbyshire. This part of the Pennine range and, with the river Dove and Dove Dale, covers the whole of the hilly country about Buxton. The geological formation of this area is millstone grit; its highest point Kinder Scout, 2,088 feet.

Here, above Buxton, you are in what I have called one of the last pockets of English landscape. As you cross the rolling moors between Barnsley and Manchester, the area of the Peak itself lies on your left. Yet even here, the land is smudged over with the grime of the industrial cities, the stone hedges black, the cottages dark and sooty. Worse, the impressive valley at Woodhead, the opening into what should be, and once was, magnificent scenery, is ruined by

View south near Llangovan, Monmouthshire
The photographer stood on high ground in dazzling early morning sunshine looking towards the Vale of Usk, only just softly emerging from white swirling mist. The dreaming, pastoral quality of this luxuriant landscape, once inhabited by the Silures, and still covered with dense forests at the time of Leland's tour (1550), immediately differentiates it from the drama of the North Welsh mountains and the bleakness of the Plynlimon slopes. The congenial aspect of these heights rightly suggests that the materials of which they are formed – sandstone and limestone – are less ancient than the unyielding rocks of Snowdonia.

The Black Mountains at
Llanthony, Monmouthshire
The photograph fully justifies
the name of these magnificent
bastions of the Welsh
highlands thrusting out into
the English border country:
it preserves the powerful
image, so particularly strong
in the narrow valley of the
Honddu, or Blackwater, of
great smooth dusky
mountain shapes filling the
sky even when viewed, as
here, from halfway up the
opposite slope. In reality, of
course, this is an Old Red
Sandstone formation and the
earth at Llanthony is a rich
Indian red.

gigantic electricity pylons alongside the reservoir. These pylons effectively split the entire area, and so dominate the scenery that you can hardly take your eyes off them.

In such distress of scenery it is probably better to go underground into the deep caverns. At Castleton, below Eldon Hill, with its Norman castle, which Scott used in his novel *Peveril of the Peak,* are Peak Cavern and Devil's Cavern. The most dramatic cavern, Speedwell, beneath the ravine of the Winnats, lies west of Castleton, near Chapel-en-le-Frith, and must be approached by boat along a channel built by the eighteenth-century lead miners. In Treak Cliff Cavern and Blue John Cavern the ancient landscape (or cavescape) has not changed. The scenery is of rock formations, stalagmites and stalactites leading to a grotto.

The Pennines, from Kinder Scout to Cross Fell in Westmorland, are separated from the foothills of the Cheviots by what is known as the Tyne Gap, which lies between the upper valleys of the river Irthing and the south Tyne. In Northumberland the foothills extend to the North Sea. In the north-west the Eden valley is the boundary between the Pennines and the mountains of the

Lake District, where Bow Fell, 2,960 feet, dominates Great Langdale. From its summit you can see, rolling away from you into the distance, the Cumbrian Mountains, lonely and remote in winter under snow and a pure, cold, blue sky. To stand here is to experience the complete, crystal, static world of the mountains.

One could hardly call the Pennines a mountain range in the same way as the Rockies or the Andes. Nevertheless, they form a north-south watershed, from which most of the larger rivers in the north of England flow. These mountainous ranges are most dramatic in the north-west, where a sharp escarpment overlooks the Eden valley. This is the Cross Fell ridge, the only real mountain range in England. Its highest peak is Cross Fell itself at 2,930 feet.

If the profile of the Pennines is low compared with other ranges, the range as a whole has glorious scenery. The Pennine Way, some 250 miles long, passes through the narrow dales of Wensleydale, Wharfedale and other Yorkshire and Derbyshire dales. The walk crosses the Border Forest National Park at Kielder in Northumberland. This forest, the largest forest area in Britain, is some 200 square miles in extent. The landscape was almost treeless until, in 1926, the planting of spruce, pine and larch began to alter the face of the countryside. Permits may be obtained for deer stalking and trout fishing in the forest, and there are points for the observation of wild life, of which the increasing number of roe deer is a delight.

The caverns and subterranean rivers, like those of the Peak, are a world of their own, lit by extraordinary lights and full of the terrors of darkness. They have been explored to great depths, for as well as climbing much pot-holing is

Mam Tor, Derbyshire
This stupendous landscape belongs to the same great backbone of rock, the Pennines, as Malham Cove (page 22), but here the wild escarpments are of shale and sandstone. Mam Tor, called 'the Shivering Mountain' from the continual fall of rocks from its vertiginous steeps, is a mountain buried under a covering of its own debris, known as screes, glitters, clitters or glyders. A great part of Mam Tor, which soars 1,300 ft above the valley, has disintegrated, taking with it part of the ramparts of a Roman fort. From this high ridge we look across the fertile valley towards the climax of the Peak, the lofty plateau of Edale Moor and Kinder Scout.

done here in such places as Ingleborough cave, near Clapham, Gaping Ghyll, a chasm over 300 feet deep, Hellan Pot and Towton Pot, near Whernside.

Because there are few lakes in the Pennines, Malham Tarn, reflecting the grey September cloudscape, comes as a surprise. You reach the lanes about the tarn by a superb mountain road, which runs from Kilnsey, where immense limestone crags hang over the road opposite Grassington Moor, to Arncliffe under Fountains Fell, the sky lifting and falling with the undulating sweep of the fells.

The Pennine Way runs through the Malham estate, which is owned by the National Trust and managed by the Field Studies Council. Any number of birds have been recorded here, from such common species as sparrow and starling, to the great crested grebe and mallard on the tarn itself, heron, pochard, shoveller and snipe, spotted flycatcher and willow warbler.

As you leave the moorland road, the wild raspberries are ripe and succulent beside the lane to the tarn, even now in early September. Beyond, and before you reach the tarn, is Malham Lings, formed by the melting of the Pennine ice cap ten thousand years ago. This lane leads through the woods to Tarn House, in which Charles Kingsley wrote part of *The Water Babies*. Near the head of the river Aire the tarn itself, which has a maximum depth of only fourteen feet, is drained by a stream which suddenly vanishes underground, rather like the disappearance of the Wye into Plunge Hole in Derbyshire.

More dramatic still is Malham Cove, a series of gracefully curved terraces of limestone clints nearly 300 feet high. Here the river Aire emerges once more into daylight. These stupendous white walls shine in a green landscape; they are the exposed bones of the land. Standing here, where Wordsworth must have stood, I could not help thinking of his poem on the place and the lines:

When giants scooped from out the rocky ground
Tier under tier, this semicirque profound.

Today the Lake District is a National Park, embracing much of Cumberland, Westmorland and the northern part of Lancashire, to which thousands of people flock each year. Indeed, I have heard Windermere described as the 'Blackpool of the Lakes'. Yet, in this area of some 700 square miles, it is still possible to escape into its remarkable and individual beauty.

If you climb the Great Gable, you can stand and look down across a landscape of small fields divided by stone hedges to the deepest lake in England. Wast Water is nearly 260 feet deep in places. The setting of the lake is wonderfully rugged and spectacular. If you follow the road from the west to the parking place at Wasdale, you are as near as you can get by car to the majestic Sca Fell peaks, which enclose the Sty Head Pass against Great Gable. In the churchyard of the hamlet of Wasdale are the graves of climbers who have died in the fells.

Helvellyn, 3,118 feet high, now has the A591 at its foot. This helps no doubt, to make it the most popular mountain for climbers, though Skiddaw, 3,054 feet,

Malham Cove, Yorkshire
The high, strangely tilting stone plateau, a jointed pavement of giant size, interrupted by great gorges known as scars, looks as arid and forbidding as a lunar landscape. Yet it excites and exalts rather than intimidates, for its wonderful archaic freshness remains intact: it is essentially as it was when there was no human eye to note its wild beauty. Eerie, empty, pallid and uneventful, the prodigious, desolate scene inspires the profoundest sense of man's predicament, a sharp awareness of the 'dread foundations' of his existence.

Mountain limestone forms discontinuous outcrops in the Mendip Hills, at Chepstow, here in the Yorkshire Pennines and in that uncanny terrain in County Clare known as the Burren, a landscape which rivals Malham in its primeval savagery. The horizontally stratified rocks took shape beneath the waters of a clear sea and their ocean origin is apparent in their composition, which consists almost entirely of the skeletal remains of marine invertebrates, fossil shells and corals. The massive blocks are in many places more than 3,000 ft thick. Once overlaid by less resistant rocks, the limestone has been exposed by millennia of driving rain and wind, and the deep vertical fissures, known as grikes or clints, by which it is traversed in all directions, drain it of all moisture, so that it is devoid of vegetation, save in the huge crevices where hart's tongue fern, wood sorrel and occasionally yellow rock roses are found.

Wrynose Pass, Cumberland
The sublime vista spread out
towards Ambleside beneath
the Wrynose rocks embraces
Langdale and Little
Langdale Tarn (from the
Icelandic *Tiorn*, a pool),
while Wansfell closes the
distance. The Romans used
this pass for their road from
Ravenglass to Ambleside.
The actual height of the
pass is no more than a few
hundred feet, but the
landscape with its softly
swelling, bare recessions and
dramatic *chiaroscuro* has all
the grandeur and a more
concentrated beauty of
configuration than many a
scene yielded by the giant
mountains of the Alps.
The shallow pool in the
rocky foreground, a little
hollow of erosion due to the
action of the ice, is
characteristic of the region.
The water is of an exquisite,
piercing blue which is not
the reflection of the sky,
although it may be enhanced
by it just as it is changed
and patterned by every
breath of wind.

Above Looking towards Howgill Fells, Westmorland Here, on the frontiers of the Lake District, the softer rock has been sculpted into smooth shapes by glaciation.

Opposite top Keswick Carles, Cumberland This stone circle, dating from the Neolithic and Bronze Ages, is comparatively simple, but it imparts a powerful magic to the heroic landscape, a vast natural amphitheatre rimmed by the bare ranges of Skiddaw and Saddleback.

Opposite bottom Little Langdale, Westmorland The emotive detail of the horse-drawn reaper conjures up pictures of agricultural life when it was still governed by centuries-old traditions of haymaking and harvesting.

is supposed to be the really 'easy' climb. Two fairly steep ascents come up to Helvellyn from Wythburn and Thirlspot, where there is a parking space. Once on the top of this range, which together Wordsworth, Sir Walter Scott, and Humphrey Davy, the inventor of the miner's safety lamp, climbed, you can see, on a fine day, into Scotland, as well as magnificent views over Red Tarn, the famous Striding Edge, and Swirrel Edge.

It is a truism to say that time and man's needs have changed the landscape. We see it happening every day. The village of Thirlmere is a case in point. Wordsworth used to go there often to meet Coleridge. They ate and drank, almost under the shadow of Helvellyn, at the village pub, The Cherry Tree, which is mentioned in his poem 'The Waggoner':

> *The mountains against heaven's grave weight*
> *Rise up, and grow to wondrous height.*

In their time Thirlmere, the lake, was smaller than it is today. The village Wordsworth knew was an agricultural community of about fourteen farms and two natural lakes. These farms were at the Dale Head and Armboth end of the valley and were built on the sites of old Norse steadings. In the late nineteenth century, however, Thirlmere as Wordsworth knew it practically disappeared under a reservoir scheme for Manchester. The pub has gone; all but two farms in the valley were drowned under water since a dam was built at the north end, which raised the water-level fifty feet. The seventeenth-century church alone remains.

26

Above Near Killin, Perthshire
Like a Claude glass the still
water at the head of Loch
Tay intensifies the image
reflected in its depths,
presenting with magically
heightened realism the
clouds wreathing the summit
of Stonachlachan and the
folds and foliage of its slopes.

Opposite Glencoe,
Argyllshire
The photograph was taken
near the head of the gorge
closed by the three jagged
peaks of the so-called Sisters
of Glencoe, Beinn Fhada,
Gearr Aonach and Aonach
Dubh. These grim rocks,
thousands of millions of
years old, are called 'meta-
morphic' because in the
course of their tortuous
history they have been
violently changed by heat
and pressure.

Scotland has over 270 mountains. A small country of about 30,000 square miles, it is one of intense grandeur. Coming up from the Border, where the land is agricultural, full of grey stone and green hills, dotted with old castles and ruined abbeys, you are presented with the most magnificent scenery in Britain, a landscape dominated by the mountain ranges of the East Grampians and the Cairngorms in the Central Highlands. In the far north are isolated mountains, enhanced and romanticized by a seascape littered with islands. Indeed, this is a truly romantic landscape, snow covered in winter and often seen through driving rain.

The Highland villages are often isolated and old fashioned, with one main street of low whitewashed cottages, a school, post office and shop and perhaps a church. Always one is aware of the mountains, their rounded summits rising above the lochs and tiny crofts – Glencoe in Argyllshire and Ben Nevis, the highest mountain in the British Isles, formidable both to climb and to contemplate.

But if the landscape of Scotland is the most magical in Britain, it is also the most terrifying. No wonder these mountains were thought to be the haunt of trolls and witches. Ben Nevis could well qualify for such legends. With sublime indifference it rears its head of loose stones and rocks over the loch at its feet. The hazardous precipices on its north-east side are torn by chasms that may hold snow all the year round.

Ben Nevis from Kilmonivaig,
Inverness-shire
The image of the Victorian
church and its cluster of
granite tombstones dwarfed
by the grand northern face
of the topmost peak of the
Grampians and the highest
mountain in Britain (4,406 ft)
movingly proclaims the
brevity not just of each of
our lives, but of the time
man has lived on earth by
comparison with the aeons
of the mountain's evolution
and existence. The length of
geological time is so immense
that we cannot grasp its
reality, yet man as a species
may endure as long as the
mountain and continue to
evolve for many more than
the mere one million years
which separate him from his
Neanderthal forebears.

The historian Macaulay describes Glencoe as 'the most dreary and melancholy of all Scottish passes – the very Valley of the Shadow of Death – even on
those rare days when the sun is bright and when there is no cloud in the sky, the
impression made by the landscape is sad and awful'. He was, of course, thinking
of the massacre of 1692, which occurred here in the pass. I disagree with him.
Its history may hold sadness, but seen on a summer's day from the shores of
Loch Leven the great upthrust of the mountain is anything but melancholy.

This is the landscape of peregrines and ravens, which nest in the crags; of
wild cats haunting cairns and forests; of the golden eagle, that royal bird, which
soars like a plane over the endless crevices and lochs of the Highlands, above
even the tree-line, above the granite mountains of Inverness-shire, which are
the most ancient in Britain. As you would expect, these are poor lands. In the
Highlands the mountains are of hard quartzite and granite. Even below the
tree-line the soil is often unfertile, needing lime and phosphate to yield at all.
Acid peat forms in undrained areas.

This montane zone, however, has its advantages. Most animal and plant life
cannot withstand its harshness, but any life that does exist up here, like the
mountain hare, which lives on heather, is in its natural state. Each winter
thousands of snow buntings fly into the Highlands from the Arctic, though
unlike the dotterel, which breeds regularly in the eastern Highlands, they do

not breed here. And if you climb Ben Lawers in spring, you will be in a rock garden of wild and rare plants, from alpine gentian to boreal fleabane, with heather everywhere to give colour to the landscape. From the summit, too, you have views both of the Atlantic and the North Sea, and closer to hand you can see down to Killin in Perthshire and the bridge over the river Dochart.

Scotland is a landscape of blazing colours – purple, violet and pink – and deep shadows. The fishing villages, such as Crail in Fife, are coloured by this warm pink and violet light which falls on their houses, many of which date from the seventeenth century. Even Bothwell Castle in Lanarkshire has a pink wash of light at some times of the day. How bathed in such light stands Elgin Cathedral in Morayshire, its ruins reflected in water across a green meadow. Deep shadows fall in Glencoe, in the Achnashellach Forest, and Glen Carron, and on the ruins of Melrose Abbey, said to be the burial place of the heart of Robert Bruce.

Stack Polly, Wester Ross
Dark reddish brown, sometimes almost black, then changing suddenly and swiftly to pale tender pink, Stack Polly is one of a number of steep, isolated mountains which, like turreted castles, keep guard over the north-west coast of Scotland. These grim, arrestingly architectural formations are of Torridon sandstone mingled with granite, shining flakes of mica, tiny glittering garnets, and white quartz that from afar looks like snow.

2 Fens, Marshes and Bogs

Fens

ANYONE who does not know the Fens can have little idea of the extraordinary quality of the sharp, brilliant light in this vast flat region of England inland from The Wash. The villages, the agricultural hutments, the sugar-beet factories seem to grow in the heightened air and the intense vibrations of light created both by the nearness of sea and the spread of inland waters.

This region, from Bedford to Hunstanton, from Lincoln to Cambridge, is one of the great productive areas of Britain. Almost a quarter of our food is grown here, from carrots to sugar-beet, from potatoes to the ubiquitous celery, in this so-called black earth. In fact, when inspected closely, the soil is more of a dark purple and is just as unexpected as the red earth of Devon. Few other areas of such rich, fertile agricultural land are left, though some can still be seen at the head of Esthwaite Water in the Lake District, and around the Norfolk Broads.

Originally the Fens were areas of waterlogged land about The Wash. This land was gradually drained, first with small beginnings under the Romans, and then more seriously in the seventeenth century. The whole area became known as the Black Fens. In the past many English villages were surrounded by such fenland, which has been drained in the last forty years. Typical of such places is another black fen near the dormitory town of Sidcup in Kent. When I was a boy it was covered in brambles and sallows, the haunt of gipsies, a very wild and watery place. Now it is a large housing estate.

Today the only true fenland left in the Fens proper is in such reserves as Wicken Fen, ten miles north-east of Cambridge. Owned by the National Trust, it covers some 700 acres and has purposely been left undrained to serve as a kind of open-air laboratory for biological study. Taking advantage of such bounty are black-tailed godwits, herons and swallowtail butterflies. From pondweed to great yellow cress, water violets and the green-winged orchid, 267 different plants have been recorded in this naturalist's paradise. Beside the river channels grow the reeds used for thatching and basket-work.

The unchanging scenery of the Fens is of black soil under vast amazing skyscapes. Before the land was drained, the fenland rivers, the Great Ouse, the Nene, the Wissey and the Welland, fell back at low tide and deposited their silts. But now Denver Sluice, that extraordinary feat of engineering, contracts the incoming water into drains, such as the strangely named Sam's Cut Drain.

The 'Roman' Bank near Leverington, Cambridgeshire This landscape of open level, thread of water and great sky is entirely man-made. The fens of south Lincolnshire and Cambridgeshire were extensively drained by means of dykes, ditches and artificial waterways by Roman engineers, and this landscape of dyke, lode and rich farmland looks much as it must have done before the drainage system of the Romans collapsed and the fens reverted to their natural state of morass in the 5th century. Thus they remained until the 7th century, when the newly founded monasteries of Ely, Thorney and Ramsey were responsible for some reclamation. But it was only in the 17th century that a determined effort was made to transform the area into productive fields.

The so-called Roman Bank runs roughly parallel to the western side of The Wash, far now from the shoreline but once, as some of the names along its course suggest – Moulton Seas End, Holbeach and Seadyke Farm – at the water's edge. Parts of the bank have proved to be pre-Conquest in date, but it is not certain that this was an entirely Roman-built embankment.

The Fens near Chatteris,
Cambridgeshire
The photograph is a late
July portrait of the Fens
when the whole flat expanse
wears the pale gold of
ripening corn. Dyke and
drain here take the place of
hedges. A road and the
Forty Foot Drain, cut in the
17th century, run along the
other side of the bank, the
water higher than the
surrounding fields. The
cottages of yellow Cam-
bridgeshire brick are set
characteristically at right
angles to the bank and the
drain, presenting a blank
wall to the north wind and
to the danger from the south
of wind-borne plague, a
danger still remembered
when the houses were built.

A road runs across the river Wissey until it comes to the crossroads at
Denver village, and from there it runs down to the river Ouse and the sluice.
Vermuyden built the first sluice only for it to be blown up by the Fen 'tigers', as
they were known. These men resented the draining because it upset their
ancient fishing-grounds. It was some time before they saw sense and allowed
it to be reconstructed. The present sluice, built by Sir John Rennie, architect of
the old Waterloo Bridge, has become as much a part of the landscape as Ely,
even though it has been remodelled since Rennie's time.

The structure broods over the endless flats of the Great Level. In summer the
sun scorches down on these unprotected wastes; in winter the fierce arctic
winds blow straight from the North Pole and chill the marrow in your bones.
Here beneath the steel superstructure of the sluice, with its ladders, its dials
and wind-gauges, and the massive bastions of stone on which it rests, the land
seems bleak and lonely, with the expanse of waters beyond. Walk across the
sluice, stand above the swollen river, and the desolation of fenland is spread out
before you. Nothing but spear-grass flourishes on the muddy banks of the man-
made rivers, the Delph and the New Bedford.

Vermuyden, when he undertook the drainage in 1631, did not realize that
by channelling the water into drains it lowered the level of the peat. As a result

the Fens gradually sank lower than the rivers into which ran the drainage channels. Later it became a landscape of windmills, which were built to lift the water away.

Always, summer or winter, you have the feeling that those who live here are constantly prepared to combat the power and danger of water. Water takes on the physical presence of the enemy. Even the little inns beside the rivers seem to be crouching back from the bank, expecting the waters to rise again and swallow them up as they did in February 1953.

Yet this landscape of straight roads, straight water channels, straight railway lines, leads the eye, at every step, towards Ely Cathedral. Whatever the danger Ely still stands in the middle of these wastes amongst its low city buildings. Inevitably the city draws you to it. Its cathedral, founded in AD 673, is a seeming impossibility here, the one completely steadfast building against the sweeping winter winds, the final spiritual answer to materialism.

As the sun rises, melting the mist, the Isle of Eels emerges out of it, a little uprising of land adorned by a small city. It draws the light upward into a luminosity which spreads over the entire landscape of the Fens. No one who

Flooded Fens near Welney, Norfolk
Despite the apparent domestication of nature in the Fens, there are still occasions when pumps fail, banks burst and the labour of centuries seems undone. The dangerous time is usually after a heavy winter, when thaw accompanied by rain sets in after snow. After a night of high wind and driving rain the Wellstream had overflowed and dykes were breached. Though the afternoon was now calm and the rain had ceased, the submerged landscape looked like a choppy sea slapping against bank and breastwork with ominous persistence.

Lincoln Cathedral from the Fens

This is the view of Lincoln from Branston Fen which de Wint preferred. It shows the spectacular sighting of the building, set not only, like Ely, on an island, but on an island which is a considerable hill. This glorious silvery image has stood against the wide cloudscape, which fills at least two thirds of the composition, for eight centuries. Until 1548 it was even more fantastic, for all three Early English towers were originally crowned with lead-sheathed timber spires, so that Lincoln Cathedral was the tallest man-made object in Britain. The central spire crashed in the 16th century and the steeples on the western towers were taken down in 1807.

has climbed to the top of the west tower of the cathedral and seen this purple light over the flat land laid at his feet will ever forget it.

This fenland continues into Lincolnshire almost up to the river Humber. The long straight road runs from Newark-on-Trent, to the elegance and delicacy of Lincoln Cathedral on its hill, along the Fosse Way and Ermine Street. The roads are lined with low, light, hawthorn hedges and, here and there, a standard tree, until you come to the dual carriageway into Scunthorpe, where you are confronted by the vast Steel Corporation factory. Flames shoot from the chimneys as if to complement the red poppies growing in amongst the green strips beside the road, running to sugar-beet factories across level fields.

This is an industrial fenland area. Yet at Normanby allotments suddenly occur in between six huge cooling towers wreathed in smoke. They form a pitiful oasis amidst the pollution of the steel works, yet a hopeful one, because they are a sign of man's vital necessities. The air here is nostalgic, permeated by the smell of old steam trains.

More remarkable still is the village of Burton upon Stather, a typical old-fashioned English hamlet not two miles away, with a saddler's shop and a minute butcher's shop. In this September the river by the inn was brown, cold, and deserted. The opposite river bank is lined with huge, overbearing electricity pylons, which seem to emphasize that the hamlet is little more than an anachronism, doomed in the midst of this industrial landscape. Burton upon Stather, with its little gardens beyond the great house of Normanby Hall, is a plea for man's need of the soil and what grows in the soil.

Marshes

Although the rich soil of the Fens makes them the most important of all flat lands in Britain, there are other landscapes that share both their beauty and their properties. The Norfolk coastline, for example, from The Wash to where it turns south, is a mixture of saltings, shingle ridges, sand dunes and marsh, which suffer from rapid physical changes. At Blakeney Point and Scolt Head the National Trust maintains two nature reserves.

The variations in plant, animal and insect life make this area an unusual location for ecological study. Winter and summer migrants alight here. Terns nest here in colonies and in the breeding season they can often be seen offering fish to their future wives. Hovering in mid-flight, then suddenly diving to catch a fish, these graceful birds are sometimes called sea swallows. Beside them will nest ringed plovers and oyster catchers. It is ironical that the oyster catcher, once a protected bird in such reserves as Blakeney Point, is now having to be culled in the same way as seals, because of their large numbers.

Cley Marsh is the largest of the Norfolk marshes. It, too, has its windmill, built in 1713 of brick and stone, with its sails attached to a wooden dome that turned with the wind. Seen here across the marshes beneath a lowering sky, the mill is the finest building in the entire flat landscape and bears witness to the fact that the eastern counties once grew major crops of milling cereals. This landscape with its flint houses is still the fenland picture. You are still aware of the closeness of The Wash and the calling of the seals which thrive there.

Further to the south, in Suffolk, is that exquisite marsh, Minsmere, a wild bird sanctuary, where the bearded tit flourishes. Owned by the Royal Society for the Protection of Birds, Minsmere is one of the largest of such marshes in England, and is set about by the small river Minsmere, which runs into the sea at Minsmere Haven. In complete contrast, about three miles south is the atomic power station at Sizewell, driving over half a million kilowatts of electricity into the Midlands along thick cables with massive pylons that everywhere cut the landscape in half.

All along this coast there are marshes behind the shoreline, like those about Southwold in Suffolk, and the Havenbeach and Town marshes beside the river Blyth. Or the long roads through the marshes of the river Deben to the shingle beach at Bawdsey, where the coastline is dotted with martello towers and where, on the pebbly beach, grows the yellow horned poppy, sea bindweed and sea thistle. Marsh marigolds, or kingcups, are the earliest flowers to bloom in marshland. These are the 'winking Mary-buds' that Shakespeare mentions in *Cymbeline*.

The salt marshes between Cley and Blakeney, Norfolk The marshes on the north Norfolk coast were created by the reverse of the process which made Dunwich part of the North Sea. Coastal accretion transformed an old line of cliffs into an inland eminence and set back the salt marshes behind a complex series of spits. These marshes, seamed by innumerable creeks and channels which fill at high tide, covered with sea lavender and samphire, the resort of the plover and redshank, form one of the most individual and enchanting landscapes in Britain.

Left Minsmere, Suffolk
Despite man-made dykes
and drains, the atmosphere
of the watery, reed-grown
domain of Minsmere is wild,
perhaps because it adjoins
the sea which shines beyond
it, apparently higher than
the morass. Minsmere is a
bird sanctuary and teems
with wildfowl, though these
are not the birds which make
the marsh memorable to the
amateur. As the walker
pushes his way through the
marshes, flags and water-
grasses, it is the garrulous
sedge warblers with their
erratic musical song and
harsh 'churr' which force
themselves on his attention,
while every now and then the
slow flight of a heron, so
mysterious and so primeval,
emphasizes the restfulness
of this tapestry of reeds,
rotting timber and water.

Still in Suffolk, beyond the quay at Orford, is Havergate Island, which is really no more than a portion of marsh cut off from the mainland by the river Ore, before it becomes the river Alde, at Aldeburgh. The island is famous for being the nesting-place of the avocet, a graceful black-and-white wader. Its long curved beak, shaped like an awl – it was once known as the awl bird – is used as a sweep to sieve out shrimps and other creatures from the shallow water.

The history of the avocet in England is remarkable. At the end of the last century it was practically extinct, for the bird was trapped for its piebald plumage, its eggs collected and its habitat destroyed by marsh drainage. However, at the end of the last war a few pairs began to nest again at Minsmere and at Havergate. They were protected by the RSPB, who use the bird as their symbol. Now about a hundred pairs nest here each year, and some fifty birds also winter on the Tamar estuary between Devon and Cornwall.

None of these marshes is as large or as famous as Romney Marsh in Kent, but the landscape here has been marred by the atomic power station at Dungeness and the pylons that go westward to the Kentish hills. And yet, not even the holiday chalet 'towns' of Camber and New Romney, Dymchurch or Littlestone-on-Sea with its sandy beach, can entirely spoil the deep quiet of the marsh behind. The smell of ripening bean fields, the cry of plovers calling beneath wide open skies, the dusty lanes I knew when I was a boy between the wars, are not entirely gone, though patterns of farming have changed. Fewer agricultural workers now live in and about what were then remote farmsteads. Not so much has changed, however, since I wrote of myself, sitting in front of

Opposite Evening on the
mudflats of the Blyth,
Blackshore, Suffolk
The limitless, enigmatic
character of this marshland
beneath its vast open sky is
most potent, most poignant
in the pause of the hour after
sunset. Familiar landmarks,
Walberswick church and the
red roofs of the village,
have been engulfed in a
monochromatic infinity. As
the light fails, a ghostly mist
rises from the river and
reedbeds. The Blyth was
once a busy waterway
carrying goods from the
former ports of Blythburgh
and Halesworth to the sea
routes to France and
Flanders. The towns
decayed with the shrinking
and choking of the river and
the destruction of neigh-
bouring Dunwich by the sea,
though Blythburgh's
splendid church survives to
brood over the marsh.

Marshland behind Orford
Beach, Suffolk
Marsh, sea, river and sky
meet and mingle in this
entrancing and wonderfully
luminous landscape. This is
Crabbe's description of the
scene:
'With ceaseless motion comes
    and goes the tide;
Flowing it fills the channel
    vast and wide,
Then back to sea, with
    strong majestic sweep
It rolls, in ebb yet terrible
    and deep;
Here samphire banks and
    saltwort bound the flood,
There stakes and sea-weeds
    withering on the mud.'
On the far side of the Ore,
encircled by the river,
Havergate Island can be
seen, breeding-ground of the
avocet. Beyond the island
lies the narrowest part of the
Orford shingle bank, a
series of great curved
concentric ridges of pebbles.

the sea with the marsh behind me: 'The marsh was blazing with heifers' eyes. The soft chewing of sedate cows was the only movement in the watermeadows. Hag's taper were yellow sentinels below green willows and tall elms. The martello tower was a guardian, tall and round, where in the past French prisoners-of-war were shut up and died of starvation. The marsh sweated in the sun. Wedges of falling and rising light were hovering over the green mat between the dykes. The air smelt of beans and brine. Shells were ringed jewels between the beach stones and, far out, a ship hauled itself between sunrise and sunset. At noon a deep mist rolled in. The skin of the sea was lifted into the air. I watched its edge creep from wave to wave. Redshank, oyster-catcher and tiny pipit flicked towards the marsh and out again, amongst the tamarisk hedges and bundles of sea-pink. Their beaks tore at the whips of horned poppies and, occasionally, a pebble rattled between their spindly legs. Their shadows were in the marram grass. Seaweeds hung from the scalp of the shore.' (James Turner, *The Crimson Moth*, 1962)

This flat marshy expanse is a dramatic change when you leave the lanes of the Weald, with their typical views of hop-fields and oast-houses. You come down into green fields, split by dykes, where small flocks of the famous Romney Marsh breed of sheep are still reared, into a flat land dominated by impressive churches in tiny villages. The boundary to the south is the road running from Appledore to New Romney, the exact line of the Rhee Wall, the old Rivi Vallum of the Romans. West and south of this 'wall' is Walland Marsh. East of Lydd is

42

another, Denge Marsh, about the town of Dungeness. These together go to make up Romney Marsh.

The whole of this flat area is bounded to the north by the Royal Military Canal, begun in 1807 as a defence against a Napoleonic invasion. To the west the river Rother flows into Rye Bay, beyond which is the ruined Camber Castle, inland from the long stretch of sand dunes.

R. H. Barham, author of *The Ingoldsby Legends*, wrote in one of them: 'The world according to the best geographers is divided into Europe, Asia, Africa, America and Romney Marsh'. Be that as it may, Romney Marsh holds all the marks of Kent, the weather-boarded houses, trim hedges, well-kept fences and poplar trees. This land has about it an air of age and use. The jackdaw and rook, the tumbling plover and the heron abide in the sometimes sombre light of dyked fields. The heron in particular adapts well to this flat land, being a large, slow-flying, dignified bird. With its wide span of grey wings and 'measured tread' in the air, the heron seems to have time to spare as it goes from one stretch of dyke to another, fitting into a tapestry of trees and rivers, of ancient churches and grey seaside towns with exquisite rightness.

The whole of the marsh can be taken in from Lympne above Stuttfall Castle. You can then see that the marsh differs from the Fens by the absence of too-long straight lines. This is one of the enchanting features of this 'map-of-land' beneath you. Though this is a drained land – it was once sea or, at least, water-logged flats – many of the dykes curve and loop. Even the short, straight roads often end in right angles, a testimony to the Romans, who began the draining of the marsh, and to the Saxons, who continued the 'inning' or cultivation.

The light here, like that of the Fens, is reflected off rich vegetation. The dykes, when uncut, are a mass of reeds and water plants. The marsh itself is vividly colourful, from the oranges and reds of willows to the emerald green of the lichen that covers the fences, though that lovely marsh plant, the mallow, has become rarer owing to drainage.

Like the South Downs, which were once covered in sheep, Romney Marsh has largely gone over to the growing of root crops and corn. Yet the characteristic buildings of the marsh – the churches, the farms, the square houses and barns – still remain. I remember them surrounded by elm trees, which now because of disease, are getting scarce.

This marsh landscape shares a peculiar feature with the fenland in that at times there appears to be no division between land and sky, the one fitting into the other like a jigsaw puzzle. Paul Nash, the artist, observed this too. He wrote in 1940: 'I have stayed on Romney Marsh and watched the eastern sky darken across the dyked flats of Dymchurch and the Channel towards the French coast as the sun set at my back, and have noticed the strange unity of sea, sky and earth that grows unnoticed at this time and place.'

Why is it that I always feel, when I drive from Taunton to Glastonbury, that I am in one of the saddest small regions in England? Sedgemoor! Is it the fact that long ago all these fields were marsh and lake, or the memory of the Battle

The Somerset Levels near Mudgley, Somerset
The marsh region of Somerset with its characteristic landscape of willow-lined ditches, called rhines in this part of the country, though as low-lying and watery as the Fens, never makes quite the same impression of an infinity of flatness. This is due not only to the fact that more of the reclaimed land is given over to rich pasturage, but that it is less rigidly organized. The drainage of these marshes was for the most part accomplished in the Middle Ages between the 12th and 15th centuries by the Abbeys of Glastonbury, Muchelney and Athelney; and the work of the medieval centuries generally shows a more irregular pattern than the unyielding parallels of road, drain and dyke in the Fens. Abrupt bends in the rhines, like that shown in the photograph, and variations in width, as well as winding ditches are all common in the Somerset Levels. The name Mudgley, like Muchelney, means big island (*ey*, island) and the place no doubt rose above the Saxon landscape of swamps.

of Sedgemoor, fought here on 6 July 1685? Is it the thought of all those young, inexperienced 'warriors' who perished in a fight that lasted no more than an hour and a half? The headquarters of King James's army was at Weston-zoyland. The site of the battle, in which the Duke of Monmouth, Charles II's illegitimate son, was defeated, is reached along a track beside the 'rhine', or ditch, at the edge of the village. Or is it Glastonbury itself, shedding the light of its legends over the marshland? Legends of Joseph of Arimathea burying the chalice which was used at the Last Supper under a spring on Glastonbury Tor, or planting his staff so that it rooted and flowered into the still-living Glastonbury Thorn? Perhaps this feeling of sadness is because Sedgemoor lacks the nobility, the width of the Fens or Romney Marsh.

Though called a moor, this is really an expanse of marsh and fenland of some 120 square miles, broken by a few isolated islands, and in winter often partially flooded. One of the characteristics of this West Country marshland is the pollarded willow, used in the flourishing trade of basket-making. If it lacks the dramatic qualities of the Fens proper, it is warmer and more intimate, scattered with redbrick farms and well-fed cattle.

Bogs

The most striking landscape of mid-Wales, after the mountains, is Tregaron Bog in Cardiganshire. The mountain road which takes you to the bog is a turning off the A438 at the village of Beulah. This stretch of twelve miles is one of the many dramatic roads in Wales, climbing into pure sheep country, rounded mountains and fir forests, and falling to the Devil's Staircase over the river Irfon. Sheep fill the valley of the river Towy when you come down into it and go up again, past Llyn Berwyn, hidden behind a screen of forest, to Tregaron Bog itself, a large, saucer-shaped area of sodden peat, clothed with scrub and sallow, of some 1,500 acres.

Bordered by the river Teifi, which has its source in the dark, sinister hollows of the Teifi Pools, it is said to be the finest example of a 'raised bog' in Europe. These raised bogs differ from ordinary valley bogs, for they develop above the valleys through the continuous growth of bog moss. Different altogether from such bogs as those of Fox Tor Mire on Dartmoor, a kind of quaking bog which does, in fact, quake and shiver as you walk on it, and will, if you are not careful to take a guide, swallow you up.

Bogs such as Tregaron, dug for their peat, are covered with wet hollows and dry hummocks. Here grow cotton-grass, deer-sedge, heathers and that curious insect-eating plant, the sundew, which thrives on sphagnum moss. The poet Crabbe, writing of it where it flourished on the marshes near Aldeburgh, described the plant:

Whose velvet leaf with radiant beauty dress'd,
Forms a gay pillow for the plover's nest.

Here, too, can be found bogbean, pondweed and butterwort, and in the bog pools insects such as craneflies, waterboatmen, which slide over the surface of the water, and water beetles.

The air of these bogs, here in Wales and on Dartmoor, is quiet and still, penetrated only by the whirring of marsh grasshoppers and the plaintive cry of curlews. Arctic geese stop at Tregaron on their migrations; the polecat lives here about the ruins of the Cistercian monastery at Strata Florida, below the Cambrian Mountains and forests. Wild ponies breed here, kingfishers inhabit the small streams, and the red kite, described by a Welsh poet as 'the living flame in the sky', has returned to nest.

3 Broads, Lakes, Lochs and Reservoirs

Broads

IN the Norfolk countryside a windmill, even one that is no longer working, a belt of trees, a church, or a redbrick cottage, instantly catches your eye and stands out against the flat landscape. In the middle of this land of woods, pasture and arable are the curious peat-dug 'lakes', the Broads.

Before the days of coal, when peat was in great demand, each such basin was connected by a straight 'cut' to the water of the nearest river to allow passage of fuel-carrying boats. The rivers of this flat land form a neat network of water lanes right up from Breydon Water behind Great Yarmouth to Norwich. These are the rivers Thurne, Ant, Bure, Yare and, to the south, the Waveney. The twelve large and twenty-four small Broads are a series of water wildernesses bordered, as if by natural fences, with lilies and tall reeds. Nearly 40,000 acres of this marshy country have been drained and are now used principally for grazing, though some is still left rough for mowing. Little corn is grown here except for a few acres round Yarmouth. Extensive reed-swamps lie between the marshes and the rivers. The uplands – you cannot call them hills – are given over to arable farming, the fields divided by hawthorn hedges, oaks, small plantations and spinneys, where pheasant and partridge are reared.

At the time of the Roman and Viking invasions this whole region was an enormous marsh reaching to Norwich, with islands of firmer soil amid the swamp. The change has been fundamental: draining, the embanking of rivers, alterations in the sea-level and the intensive cutting of peat have created the landscape we see today. Only a memory of the old thriving industries is left, although there has been a small revival of reed-cutting for thatching of ricks and houses. The reeds are cut in winter in alternate years and are loaded on to boats. They are then taken to a staithe to be stacked. Osiers, too, are still cut for basket-making.

Although the Montagu's harrier and marsh harrier are no longer so abundant as once they were, the Broads have become nature reserves. You can still hear the 'chunking' of bearded tits, or 'reed pheasants' as they are called. Amongst the reeds the bittern still booms. The waters are inhabited by the great crested grebe, migratory spoonbills, flocks of black tern, grasshopper warblers and sedge warblers, and even the osprey has been known to frequent the area. There is a rich variety of insects, from the swallowtail butterfly and local moths

River Thurne, Norfolk Broads
Recent research by Dr J. M. Lambert, Joseph Jennings and C. T. Smith has established that the enigmatic region of reed-fringed lagoons and sluggish rivers which we call the Broads was created during the Middle Ages by centuries of deep peat-cutting. One of the peculiarities of the Broads, which led to a renewed attempt to solve the mystery of their origin, is that they are not, as might seem, broadenings of rivers, but that they lie to either side of the rivers, connected to them by man-made dykes. The river Thurne is seen at the point where it passes close to Martham Broad. Medieval account rolls prove that turf was cut at Martham throughout the 14th century. The photograph is expressive of the visual delights of this wide-horizoned scene, of the exciting light which gives drama to its sallow-dotted expanses, and of the emphatic character of the windmills, which start up from the low tranquil landscape to remind us of the efforts made to drain the marshes before electric pumps were invented.

like the 'wainscots', to the two rare dragonflies which breed nowhere else, the *Aeshna isosceles* and the *Coenagrion armatum*.

Here, too, in the undisturbed waters of certain Broads the staghorn weed is found. It is probably true to say that the Broads are the last home of such plants as water soldier and cowbane, while the fen orchid and round-leaved winter-green grow in remote mossy fen country between the waters. The air of the Broads is pervaded by waves of the sickly scent of meadowsweet and the sharp tang of water mint in the early morning.

An animal still inhabiting the Broads is the South American coypu, a rat-like creature easily mistaken, when swimming, for an otter. Introduced here for fur-farming in the 1930s, a few escaped into the marshes and multiplied to such an extent that they became pests. The hard winter of 1962 severely reduced the numbers of these escapees, but they were so well adapted to the landscape, living off roots of reeds, sedges, rushes, pondweeds, mussels and snails, that they survived.

Beneath a sky as open and long-horizoned as that of the Fens the waters are bounded by mile after mile of tall marsh thistles. At every turn of a river a new landscape opens out. In the expanse of unspoiled country, away from the tourist boating centres, such as Wroxham and Potter Heigham, few buildings are to be seen – a marshman's cottage, perhaps, and here and there a farm shed or a boathouse. Since the eighteenth century the cottages have been built of red brick and clay lump, keeping them warm in winter and cool in summer. Fifty years ago the only craft to be seen on the water were wherries, taking cargoes of

Broads on the border of Suffolk and Norfolk
The palisades of reeds, which as much as mere and river determine the image of the Broads, arouse an over-whelming sense of remote-ness. It is a memorable experience (despite the mosquitoes) to walk along the edge of a great Broadland reedbed or to lie in its depths in a flat-bottomed boat, soothed by the unceasing rustle and whisper of the undergrowth, diverted by the clink of bearded tits and the gentle chirp of reed warblers. The great reedmace and common reed, sweet flags and water soldiers can all be seen in the photograph, while in the distance rise a typical Broadland mill and the mysterious silhouette of Burgh Castle.

Burgh Castle, Suffolk
We are looking past the massive southern wall and bastions of the Roman fort into a flat expanse of grazing marsh. When this fort was built in *c.* 290, the Broads did not exist, although Breydon Water, an estuary almost cut off from the sea by a sand spit, looked much as it does today and provided an ideal harbour for the naval squadron which, together with the regiments garrisoned in the fortress, was to meet the menace of raiders from across the North Sea. For Burgh Castle, called Gariannonum by the Romans, was built under Carausius, Admiral of the *classis Britannica*, as one of the Forts of the Saxon Shore, the series of coastal defences between The Wash and The Solent. The great quadrangular structure covers more than five acres, and three of its mighty walls have survived for seventeen centuries, proof of the strength of the Roman mortar in which the local flint and alternating courses of tiles are embedded.

corn, coal and timber to Yarmouth, Lowestoft or inland towns. Now the wherries have almost disappeared. Other boats have taken their place.

In summer each Broad is alive with craft of every description, sails of every colour. But out of season nothing interrupts the view across the expanse of water but the lonely black drainage mills. From the mill at Horsey you can see across Horsey Mere and out to sea, though the mill itself was struck by lightning in 1943 and is no longer used for drainage. In autumn or winter the loneliness of these level stretches is profound and often disquieting. One has the feeling of being in a vast web of water from which there is no escape.

Through this land of marsh, woods and reeds the river Bure runs for thirty miles without a lock. If you stand on the single-span bridge at Wroxham, you will see in front of you the most beautiful of all Broads, Wroxham. It is a mile long and over one hundred acres of water. Here the tangle of waterways, fens and marshes are not easily negotiated without a map. To the north is Barton Broad on the river Ant, and Hickling Broad, renowned for its pike. The waters of Hickling, like those of Horsey, are above the level of the drained alluvial land, separated from it by embankments. The greater part of this Broad is a national nature reserve, but river craft have free access.

One of my favourite views is that of St Benet's Abbey, which lies east of Ranworth Broad on the river Bure. A ruined windmill stands behind what is left of the abbey gate right at the water's edge. At evening, when the sun falls on the water, the marsh and the ruined turreted gatehouse turn a dark, forbidding colour. But before darkness finally sets in it is possible to come south by Fleet Dyke to the village of South Walsham, where there is a private Broad below the rising woods.

My other favourite spot is Reedham Ferry where the chain car-ferry takes you over the river Yare. It can be an eerie experience to cross the river on the last ferry boat, at dusk, in winter, when the reeds are dry, yellow and filled with wind. The river is narrow at this point and once across to the other side you are in Halvergate Marshes, which were reclaimed from the sea and divided by dykes, on which rest the remains of the old drainage windmills.

With the growth of towns such as Yarmouth and Lowestoft the water of the Broads has an added importance. Yarmouth, for example, is supplied with water from the lovely Ormesby Broad, while Fritton Decoy Lake has been converted into a reservoir for Lowestoft. Filby and Ormesby Broads are no longer accessible by water since the Muck Fleet is now silted up, but they can be seen very well from the roads which cross them on causeways.

The scenery of the Broads is, as much as anything else, the vegetation growing beside the waters, and the animals and insects living in and on them. The waters themselves, enclosed with thick copses of sallow and alder, reflect the colour of the vast open skies above them. It is not only a landscape of flat water but of long streaming rivers with only a slight fall to the sea.

At Burgh Castle, near the great stretch of Breydon Water, under a full moon, the tapestry of countryside and Broads is illuminated by the same light which fell on this land when it was one huge estuary. Standing on the beach one thinks back to the loneliness of St Benet's Abbey in the marshes, to the herons at Reedham, to the desolate churches and the many round towers of this land, pointing like fingers into the night sky.

Lakes

The contrast between the Broads and the Lake District, which lies between the Pennines and the sea in Cumberland, Westmorland and Lancashire, is remarkable. Unlike the flat Norfolk landscape the Lakes are set against a background of mountains, some of them the highest in England.

The Lakes attract visitors for many reasons – for the astonishing beauty of the landscape, for the sailing, for example on Windermere, or for its literary associations. About 900 square miles of this region are now a National Park, filled with memories of Wordsworth and the Lake Poets.

Grasmere, Cumberland
There is scarcely a knoll or crag or coppice in this scene, apart from the lake itself, patterned and fretted by the wind, which has not been immortalized in the writings of William and Dorothy Wordsworth. Gray's description of the scene of the photograph, viewed from a higher point, is perhaps less familiar:

'The bosom of the mountains spreading here into a broad basin, discovers in the midst Grasmere Water; its margin is hollowed into small bays, with eminences, some of rock, some of the soft turf, that half conceal and vary the figure of the little lake they command . . . hanging enclosures, cornfields and meadows green as an emerald, with their trees and hedges and cattle, fill up the whole space from the edge of the water; and just opposite to you is a large farmhouse at the bottom of a steep smooth lawn, embosomed in old woods which climb halfway up the mountain-sides and discover above a broken line of crags that crown the scene.'

In fact it is probably true to say that Wordsworth began the present-day tourist invasion of the Lake District when he wrote his *Description of the Scenery of the Lakes* in 1810. He spent sixty years at Hawkshead, Grasmere and Rydal Mount. He and his wife are buried in Grasmere churchyard. His sister Dorothy, however, best describes the landscape in her *Journals*. She and William came to live at Dove Cottage at Grasmere at the head of Lake Windermere in 1799. Her diary entry for 31 January 1802 reads: 'We walked round the two lakes, Grasmere was very soft and Rydal was extremely beautiful from the western side. Nab Scar was just topped by a cloud cutting it off as high as it could be cut off, made the mountain look uncommonly lofty.' Two days later she noticed a curious effect of the light, so typical of the landscape in stormy weather. 'There was a purplish light upon Mr Oliff's house, which made me look to the other side of the vale when I saw a strange stormy mist coming down the side of Silver How of a reddish purple colour. It soon came on heavy rain.'

Wast Water, Cumberland
Wast Water, lying like a
stretched silken cloth with
scarcely a wrinkle in the
shadow of the Great Gable,
Scafell Pikes, Sca Fell and
The Screes, is the sternest
and most spectacular of the
Lakes and it is the deepest.
At the narrower end, at
which we are looking, the
lake is 258 ft deep. With its
harsh skyline of volcanic
rock and sculptural, marble-
like cliffs Wast Water is
totally different from wooded
Grasmere. It comes closer
than any of the Lakes to the
primitive state of a glacial
mere. Its water is excep-
tionally pure and except for
char, minnows and stickle-
backs, supports little life,
while the thin poor soil on
its margins is unsuitable for
agriculture or grazing,
though a rare cinquefoil
grows in the deep gullies of
The Screes.

The southernmost lake is Windermere, the largest lake in England, being over ten miles long. The wooded shores of the lake change character from one end to the other, running from a mild south into the cold of the mountains at its northern end. It no longer matters where you go from here, it is apparent that the gentle south, the flatness of the Midlands, is gone. You are in more danger-ous and more awesome landscapes.

Beyond the Kirkstone Pass rises Helvellyn and, as yet, one is not into deepest Lakeland. This is approached by one of the most dramatic ways to the west, via Hard Knott Pass in Cumberland. A curving road will bring you to Wast Water, set in the most majestic and sombre scenery. Apart from being the deepest English lake, 258 feet in places, it is surrounded by formidable screes, deep walls of rubble and the majestic peaks of Great Gable and Scafell. The National Trust owns 40 acres on Scafell Pikes, given as a War Memorial for the Lake District in 1920. Near Styhead Pass there are another 1,200 acres above the 1,500-foot mark, presented as a War Memorial to club members in 1923 by the Fell and Rock Climbing Club.

Buttermere lies in beautiful Lakeland scenery and is a fine climbing centre. Stand on Green Crag and look down the walls of the valley to Crummock Water. Here is Scale Force, the highest waterfall in the Lakes. To the north is Bassenthwaite Lake, the most northerly of the Lakes, lying on the flight-path of many varieties of birds from the wild-fowl breeding grounds at Morecambe Bay to the Solway Firth at the end of Hadrian's Wall. Much of Bassenthwaite, however, is private property. It is all the more depressing that in order to widen the A66 road a section of the lake landscape is being devastated. Already, as I write, the screen of trees near the site of the old railway station has gone, and shortly the lake-edge of the hill-fort at Castle How is to be cut away. It was here beside the Lake that Tennyson sat and wrote:

I heard the water lapping on the crag
And the long ripple washing in the reeds.

And so you come back east to the beauty of Derwent Water, oval in shape, and surrounded by round-headed mountains, broken only to the north-west by the long valley of Borrowdale, which takes the river Derwent out through Bassenthwaite Lake. Haweswater in Westmorland was once a lake. It is now a reservoir, as is Thirlmere, near Blea Tarn, the deepest tarn in Lakeland.

Most people, I think, having once visited the fantastic scenery of the Lakes settle for one lake above all others. My choice would still be Rydal Water, the smallest and most intimate of the lakes, sheltered by Rydal Fell. It was here in 1826 that Wordsworth bought the plot of land still known as Dora's Field, and planted it with daffodils for his daughter; it was here, too, at Rydal that Wordsworth died.

Popularity has destroyed much of the mystery of this landscape and spoiled the wonder. It is to this mystery and wonder that somehow we have to come back. Only in winter, when the lakes are ice-blue below the snow-laden upper rides of the mountains, does the essential haunting quality of the landscape

Lake Dinas, Caernarvon-
shire
Like some of the Lake
District waters Llyn Dinas is
thought to be a drowned
river valley which was
perhaps once linked with
Llyn Gwynant. Though
skirted by a tourist-used
road, this romantic lake with
its legendary associations
with Merlin and its amazing
indigo colour makes an
unforgettable impression of
desolate yet uplifting
grandeur. The mountain
louring in the background is
Snowdon.

return. Or on an early summer's morning in the village of Rosthwaite, for
example, across the chessboard fields and up the valley of Borrowdale, where
the magnificent peaks and fells unfold in the distance. Or at dawn, beneath the
silver birch trees beside Ullswater, where the purple depths of the mountains
opposite lie hidden below the sunlit peaks beyond. At such moments the upthrust of these mountains, with the black inky depths of the lakes below, appear
out of the mist, out of the rain, in all their ancient terror.

Much of the old landscape has been quite transformed by the huge plantations of the Forestry Commission. The upper valley of Ennerdale, for example, where once there was hardly a tree, is now clothed with deep curtains of
conifers. And the shores of Tarn Howes are now completely surrounded by
these 'foreign' trees.

If you wish to discover the greatest treasures of flora and fauna, you will have
to penetrate into the wilder parts of Cumberland and Westmorland. Deep in

the mountains and beside the lakes you may still find bee orchid, pink sundew, bog asphodel and wild scabious. Herons are often to be seen by the sides of lakes, while the curlew and the plover make their nests in the boggy lands. The great crested grebe inhabits these waters, and occasionally the osprey and the great grey shrike are to be seen. The red deer, the fox and the badger have retreated to the remoter parts of the area.

Today few of the old slate 'hedges' still remain. These were constructed of large thin slates, like headstones to graves, their edges touching, fencing off fields and roads. You might still find bits of such hedges round Coniston and Hawkshead, about the gardens of the old thick-walled cottages. Many of the roads in the National Park are still walled with stone and look well.

The slate industry itself is far from dead. It is thriving in the mines at Honister, for example. Buttermere Green is reputed to be the best slate in the world, quarried from the green slate screes in the midst of a forbidding landscape which is dominated by the colossal sweep of Honister Crag. Millions of years ago natural forces ground out these great slopes; volcanic eruptions and the weight of the Ice Age worked upon them to effect what we see today.

The largest of the Welsh lakes is Bala in Merionethshire, five miles north of the Aran Peaks, the highest of which is almost 3,000 feet. Surrounded by heather-clad hills with a backdrop of mountains this lake deservedly earned its Welsh name, Llyn Tegid, which means 'the Lake of Beauty'. Like the river Dee, which runs through the lake, the waters abound with many different kinds of fish, including the gwyniad, a small white-scaled fish.

Then there is the lovely Tal-y-llyn, already mentioned in the chapter on mountains, and the tiny Cwmystradllyn, which is reached from Tremadoc on the A4085 road to Caernarvon. The valley here, Cwm Pennant, is one of the loveliest in Wales, a grouping of water-meadows crossed by small streams, ending abruptly in an enormous wall of almost impassable mountain.

These smaller lakes have a more intimate charm, quite different from the sweeping grandeur of Windermere. Like Dozmary Pool on Bodmin Moor, where according to Tennyson, King Arthur embarked on his journey to Avalon in the barge of the Three Queens, and Loe Pool, also in Cornwall, these lakes possess a special quality, which adds to the peace and quiet and, above all, the width of landscape.

Lochs

Most of the Scottish lochs are long, narrow and deep. The deepest is Loch Morar reaching 1,017 feet, but there are also the sea lochs, like Loch Ewe, created by glaciers reaching the coast. You would think, from looking at any atlas, that Scotland is nothing but a mass of water, interspersed with moorland, high mountains and golf links. There must be hundreds of main lochs, both sea and fresh water, to say nothing of the smaller lochans above the Great Glen.

Loch Assynt, Sutherland
The landscape of the Central Highlands, however imposing, is at certain seasons so hostile, so acid in colouring, that its wildness depresses rather than exalts the spirits. But towards the west the softer, more poetic light of a moister, warmer climate informs scenes of picturesque splendour with a strange and irresistible charm. Loch Assynt in the far north-west is a place of magic. The sheet of water lies between sandstone mountains, one of them, seen in the photograph, the noble Ben More Coigach, a name redolent of Gaelic enchantment, a name like that of some legendary knight. The firs on the island, upon which this composition so largely depends for its effect, are unusual in this countryside of bare rocks and moorland scrub and lend a quite unexpected, exciting Japanese flavour to the northern landscape. But if well-grown trees are rare on the shores of Loch Assynt, they are noted for alpine flowers and ferns.

More like tarns, these are mostly circular, high in the mountains and often difficult to reach.

So it is hardly possible to do more than describe a few of the less well-known and smaller lochs before they, and the coasts of northern Scotland, are ruined by the oil companies. Nothing could be more wonderful than to stand above Loch Craignish, looking towards the distant mountains. The loch, on the west coast of Argyllshire, is six miles long. Near at hand the water is a vivid blue, paling into a white brilliance where the sun strikes it, contrasting with the green of its low islands and, in July, the yellow of cut hayfields on the far slopes.

You are aware, too, that but a stone's throw away is the longest of all Scottish Lochs, Loch Awe, which at its southern end is narrow, only broadening out below the peaks of Ben Cruachan, 3,689, and Ben Eunaich, 3,242. This is grand scenery indeed! From Ben Cruachan, with its eight summits, a large area of Argyllshire can be seen, Loch Awe itself, the roads running on either side bordered on the west by the Forest of Interliever, the huge hydro-electric 'factories' and dams, and that tiny water, Loch Aich. North-east from Loch Awe, beyond Kilchurn Castle at its head and up Glen Orchy, is Loch Tulla, famous for its salmon and trout. Loch Tulla lies in Rannoch Moor, a wide moorland area of some twenty miles, broken up by green hillocks, granite boulders, peaty tarns and its own small lochs, beyond which rise the mountains of Glencoe. It was to this moor that David Balfour and Alan Breck escaped from the dragoons in Stevenson's novel *Kidnapped*. This is an entirely wild landscape of water and high hills, seen at its most dramatic under snow.

There is a wonderful walk, along a right-of-way private track, from Loch Tulla to the minute Loch Dochard. At Tulla red deer come to the Forest Lodge to be fed, and here under Black Mount ospreys have been seen fishing the loch. In this empty vastness live, too, the badger, otter and wildcat, and there is an impressive variety of bird life from capercailzie to greenshank, which nest in the hills, but come to feed at the shore with oyster catchers and wagtails. Loch Dochard is remote and grand, orchestrated by land streams falling down the encircling mountains.

Westward of Loch Shin and south-west of Loch Assynt, with its endless system of caves and its ruined castle of Ardvreck, is the small Loch Ganive in Sutherland. The loch lies below Suilven, the Pillar Mountain, that raises its pink sandstone over grey gneiss, some 2,399 feet high. Its summit is reflected in the waters of Cam Loch, with its wild cascade of water flowing into the larger Loch Veyatie.

The road from Ullapool, on Loch Broom, to Drumrunie, ten miles away, shows you the glory of loch and mountain scenery. With the jagged face of Ben More Coigach to the north, it skirts two lochs, Lurgainn and Bad a' Ghaill, turning right to Inverkirkaig, below Inverpolly Forest, with its fine view of Suilven. On the right is that favourite resort of rock climbers, Stack Polly, or the Stack of the Bog, with its long west-to-east ridge.

Certain pictures remain in the mind, such as Loch Affric surrounded by its ring of trees; the great dam at Loch Lyon with Stuchd an Lochain under snow

Top Loch Lomond, Stirlingshire
Smollett was born at Dalquarn House near Loch Lomond and extolled the loch, its richly wooded shores and islands and its abundance of fish, as vying with Arcadia. The photograph, taken on a stormy late autumn morning from the northern end of the loch, preserves a moment which emphasizes the romantic character of the landscape, a moment when a burst of sunlight from the sombre sky dazzles the water, and an empty boat accentuates the loneliness of the limpid recessions. On the left Ben Lomond rises in deep shadow, and the glittering distance is closed by a shoal of islands.

Bottom Loch Long, Argyllshire
Loch Long is a saltwater lake, though the place from which we are looking, Arrochar, is at least 20 miles from the sea. The origin of the loch is obscure, but it is thought that at the beginning of the Glacial Period it was a deep mountain gorge, slowly metamorphosed into its present form by the action of ice and the influx of saltwater. William and Dorothy Wordsworth were struck by the solemnity and stillness of the scene, and when the photographer pointed his camera towards the fiery sunset on a May evening more than 150 years later, it was the extraordinary smoothness of the water and the brooding melancholy of the mountains, the Lilliputian insignificance of the silhouetted anglers on the broken jetty, and above all the deep hush of the vast landscape which he wished to record.

59

Loch Voltas, Lewis
Loch Voltas is one of many
little rock tarns, dotted like
mirrors across the strange
black moor, a peat bog on
the island of Lewis. Sometimes the loch-reflected
image of the moor is blacker
than the bog itself;
sometimes the water is as
placid and colourless as
glass; sometimes it is vivid
aquamarine.

in the distance; black tern fly-catching over the shallow, lowland Kilconquhar
Loch. The remote Loch Fannich in its ring of high mountains and deer forests,
and Loch Maree with its national nature reserve and the peaks of Slioch
looking down on you like a series of pink pyramids over grey gneiss and where
pine marten live, and deer, and eagle and peregrine falcon hover.

There are scenes which are unforgettable, like the road twisting round Loch
Ard overhung by the north face of Ben Lomond; or Loch Watten, where you
can fish for brown and sea trout; the rowan trees of Loch Sionascaig in Wester
Ross, lying in its circle of blue mountains; or the golden eagle over the Five
Sisters of Kintail, under light cloud above Loch Duich.

Reservoirs

There will always be controversy over the necessary creation of artificial reservoirs to supply our larger towns and cities. Several natural lakes have already been turned into reservoirs, like Lake Dulyn, the Black Lake, in Snowdonia, which lies under colossal towering crags, supplying Llandudno with water.

Despite criticisms, many of these artificially created reservoirs add distinctiveness to a landscape once the newness has worn off. From the town of Rhayader, for instance, you come to the Elan Valley reservoirs which serve Birmingham. It is arguable that this is an artificial landscape, man-made; but, then, almost every part of the landscape reflects the work of man in one way or another. Driving round these reservoir lakes for some eight miles, you follow the road across the dams and under great hanging mountains. When the lakes are full, the water pours over the dams in magnificent curtains, reflecting the light of rock and woodland, and filling the valley with the roar of falling water.

Now that time has worked on these artificial lakes with their concrete surrounds, they have become part of the landscape. True, it is a different landscape from the old one that was flooded. Small pumping stations, like those at the reservoir at Layer-de-la-Haye, near Colchester, in Essex, not so long ago brash and new, have now become integrated with the low, sloping fields and look like miniature temples built out on piers in the water. Rudyard Lake in Staffordshire, constructed to supply the Trent and Mersey Canal, looks like a lowland loch in its pastoral setting with woods coming down to the shore, broken here and there by red cliffs.

Siblyback, one of Cornwall's reservoirs, creates a splendid diversion amongst the low green hills of the moors near the Cheese Wring. The new Crowdy reservoir lies like a mirror below the rock uplift of Rough Tor. Before it was dammed and flooded this was nothing but marsh and bog where sheep and cattle often strayed and were lost. The Burrator reservoir, which supplies Plymouth, lies below Sheepstor, and was created by damming the river Meavy. Dartmoor is here beautiful in its harshness, and the grey eminence of Sheepstor is echoed in the white spoil heaps of the china clay mines on Lee Moor.

One of the most beautiful of all reservoirs is Lake Vyrnwy in Montgomery-shire. The creation of the five-mile stretch of water serving Liverpool involved the drowning of a whole village. Yet even though the setting is austere, when one stands above the water at sunset and looks down on the darkening trees, on the tall shores of the lake and on the crimsoned water, even this 'desecration' seems worth while. In short, if artificial reservoirs destroy a landscape which has been hallowed by antiquity, they replace it with definite beauties of their own.

4 Downs and Hills

Downs

An hour's run from London is the warm, intimate landscape of the South Downs in Sussex. These smooth, well-wooded, sweeping hills are not high in themselves, though from sea-level they often look higher than they are. From Old Winchester Hill in the west, to Firle Beacon and the Long Man of Wilmington in the east, they stretch for about fifty miles. Often lonely and deserted, like the moors in Yorkshire or Cornwall, these downs stand invitingly above the sea towns of Worthing, Brighton and Littlehampton.

To go up the long walk to Cissbury from the village of Sompting, with its church with a 'Rhenish Helm', by way of a narrow lane between flint walls, known in Sussex as a 'twitten', is to come into the landscape of deep downland farming. Yet the smell of the sea still breathes in the valleys and the uplands of these low hills, covered, here and there, with ancient Roman camps and belts of trees.

Chanctonbury Ring, the finest of these man-planted belts, is high above the village of Washington. Beech trees mark the site of a prehistoric hill-fort. Not so long ago you could stand here and look out to a land cropped by sheep and Highland cattle. Today much of the downs is cultivated for cereals, thus changing the entire colour of the landscape.

From the vantage point of Chanctonbury Ring you can see the valley of the river Adur and, standing on its hill above Shoreham-by-Sea, Lancing College Chapel, built in 1848. The chapel is built of sandstone with a chalk and stone roof, the very stuff of downland, but most of the other school buildings are faced with split flint. Flint is a wonderfully strong and weather-resistant facing material, which today would be very costly to use, since it takes an expert to split the flints exactly. Many of the villages below the downs, however, such as Bramber, with its ruined castle, and Beeding, have cottages faced with whole flints.

In winter this downland is scored with cold winds blowing through the long grasses about the dewpond at Chanctonbury Ring, or in the open corridors of that other prehistoric fort at Cissbury. In summer the sun is reflected off the rounded hills into the valleys and half-dried-up dykes of the marshland below. And to the east is the Long Man of Wilmington, standing like a huge skier with staves in either hand, in a hollow of Windover Hill.

The downs are chalk hills dating back to prehistoric times. Neolithic man

Top The South Downs in winter, from Mount Caburn, Sussex
A pale morning sun illumines the snow-scattered downs where winter has deepened the solitude and repose of the scene. The gorse showing darkly in the foreground of the picture is evidence of a sandy soil, which here takes the place of the loam that produces the short sweet turf of the downs. Mount Caburn lies to the east of Lewes and the view preserved by the camera is that commanded for some three centuries by an important Iron Age fort.

Bottom The South Downs above Glynde, Sussex
Of all the chalk downs which are so characteristic of England those of Sussex are the most beautiful in contour, presenting a series of smooth, swelling curves that echo the rounded shapes of the sheep which graze upon them. Once having left the field with the sheep we are on the close, springy, peculiarly English turf of the downs, composed of little hillocks of sweet thyme, tufts of golden potentilla, harebells and the spiky squinancywort. The circular tree-grown depression in the middle distance is a dew pond, a common incident in a landscape where drainage is almost wholly subterranean.

63

used the flints he found or mined here for tools and weapons. Arrowheads and
flint-scrapers can still be found, if you are lucky, at such places as Cissbury or
Lancing Ring.

In the grassland between cultivations lives a large variety of insects and plants.
I have sat in fields carpeted with cowslips, or in gardens of harebells on the hill
tops all along the 'range'. Milkwort, campion and bee orchid can still be found,
though the wild orchids of my youth are rarer now because of the increased
growing of corn. The corncockle which ought to be found here, and once was
common in all cornfields, has mostly been sprayed out of existence. It has
become one of a large number of rare plants in England.

These rolling downland spaces are populated with butterflies and burnet
moths. I have walked on the slope of a downland valley in summer and seen
the grass covered with these red, black and green moths which we called
'Mother Shipton'. It is an unforgettable sight. Perhaps the loveliest and most
familiar butterfly – so redolent of summer on these chalk hills – is the tiny chalk
hill blue. One of the stranger creatures to be found all over downland is the old
Roman edible snail, which builds its shell from the chalk by means of a special
gland.

One of the effects of the decline of the famous South Down sheep is the
abundance of scrub such as juniper, which also benefited from the destruction
of rabbits by myxamatosis. Adders and grass snakes are less common now than
they used to be, but occasionally they can be found basking on a stone in the hot
sun. Above all it is the song of the lark that is the real voice of the South Downs,
filling the air above cornfield and hilltop, above ancient fort and dewpond,
above the marshland dykes and clustered villages all spring and summer long.
They are your constant companions as you walk the South Downs Way, the
turf beneath your feet scented with thyme and tiny heather. The eighty-mile
path runs from Beachy Head, near Eastbourne, to South Harting, on the
Hampshire border. In April 1974 the last link was completed when a bridge
was opened over the river Adur at Botolphs in Sussex, with the object of saving
walkers and horse riders a long detour by road.

The North Downs in Kent, like the South, are not a continuous 'range' of hills.
They stretch from the western boundary of the county for ninety-five miles
from the white chalk cliffs at Dover and the famous headland, Shakespeare's
Cliff, to Farnham in Surrey. These downs, the 'backbone of Kent' are broken
by valleys of the rivers Darent, Medway and Stour. They cut right across the
county, with the chalk plateau to the north and to the south the Weald.

Everywhere on hillsides and above rivers are discreet plantations of ash and
chestnut, much prized in Kent. Grown as a crop, they are cut in rotation after
fifteen, eighteen or twenty years, and the wood is used for hurdles, fencing or
poles in the hop-fields. After harvesting in early autumn the hops are dried in
oast-houses, and, standing on the hills, you can look down on them with their
brick bases, red-slated roofs and white wooden wind cowls. Today many of
them have been turned into dwelling houses.

Kent is the largest hop-growing area in the south of England, though they are also grown in Worcestershire and Herefordshire, where the oast-houses are square and the fields are called 'hop-yards'. To work in these fields when the flowers are ripe and being pulled down before being taken to the oast-houses, is to experience a wonderful feeling of drowsiness and well-being.

Opposite Burnham Beeches, Buckinghamshire

Most common varieties of bird are to be found in Kent, but one whose disappearance I much regret is the wryneck. This curious bird can turn its head completely round on its neck, but it is a difficult bird to see, for the bronze and grey mottling of its plumage is a wonderful disguise against the bark of a tree. When, as a boy, I lived in a house in Staplehurst, near Maidstone, I would often hear its call in the old orchard, 'quee, quee, quee', and I would go to the nesting-box we had put there to look at its white eggs. Now only a few pairs remain in Kent.

'The Garden of England', as Kent is known, is sheltered by downland, with orchards of cherries, plums and apples in glorious display of their spring blossom. The farmhouses, almost always lying in the centre of such orchards, are built in Kentish ragstone, from the ragstone ridge which rises 800 feet above Sevenoaks. The colour of this landscape, with the white chalk, the orchards and the hop-gardens, is white and green with splashes of red from the house tiles.

The Berkshire Downs are crossed by an ancient road, the Berkshire Ridge Way, which runs on into Wiltshire and so to Stonehenge. These downs the highest chalk downs in England, rise to almost 1,000 feet at Inkpen Beacon and Walbury Camp. From this beacon the great swathe of bare chalk ridges and lush valleys is laid out like an enormous green-and-white bull's-eye sweet, while in and about the village of Inkpen itself grow wild tulips, lilies and daffodils. It is suggested that these flowers, growing wild, were first brought over from Asia Minor by the Knights Templar.

Walking high above the valleys which these downs enfold you come at last to that picture-in-landscape, the Uffington White Horse across the Vale of the same name. It is believed to date from 1000 BC. From the air the road beneath looks like a white line under a signature, and below is the flat-topped Dragon Hill, where St George is said to have killed the monster.

Most buildings in the Berkshire towns are brick, but occasionally, in the past, Sarsen stones were brought in from downland and incorporated into chalk or cob walls. Wattle and daub, as in East Anglia, was much used, and thatch in place of tiles is still to be seen.

On these downs you may come across the lovely purple pasque flower near Lowbury Camp, and by the river Loddon there grows the Loddon Lily. All over the downs are the 'gallops' of the racehorses which are trained on these uplands. They will come over the skyline, a long string of them, out of the mist of early morning and back down the lanes to their stables. They are as much a signature of Berkshire as are the few sheep still on the downs, or the coffee-cream fields of after-harvest.

Above The White Horse,
Uffington, Berkshire
The most ancient of such
hill figures, the eerie sinuous
creature leaping overhead
dates from *c.* 100 BC, the
period when the horse cult
first became prominent.

Opposite Stonehenge,
Salisbury Plain, Wiltshire
The stupendous Bronze Age
monument matches the vast,
open landscape in grandeur,
yet is not truly part of it:
only the finest fabric was
considered worthy of so
great a temple, and it was
built of imported materials.

The Wiltshire Downs are long, wide, open stretches of landscape crossed by rolling roads with enormous views on either side. They are divided by the delightful Vale of Pewsey, through which runs the Kennet and Avon Canal. Salisbury Plain, the other half of the downs, lies to the south of the Vale.

In these vast open spaces the ancient monuments, the Grey Wethers and Sarsens, stand in the fields and on the bare downs like human figures frozen for all time, marking the way to Avebury and Stonehenge and Silbury Hill. To touch these Sarsens, or the Slaughter Stone at the entrance of the Circle at Stonehenge, is to be taken back into a time when the landscape we now see, modern roads, modern agricultural machinery, did not exist.

One of the best places to look down on this modern landscape is Hackpen Hill, where the downs roll away timelessly, south and east of Marlborough and Salisbury Plain. A land of huge agricultural machines, reaping, ploughing and sowing, a kind of Mid-West landscape with few trees, it has the colour of its cornfields, golden palettes surrounding the greyness of its ancient stones. The

Salisbury Plain near Deptford, Wiltshire
The lonely, undulating chalk uplands are marked with sheep walks and with the traces of Celtic and Saxon cultivators. This is one of the most distinctive types of landscape in England with its waterless valleys and white scars. The farm buildings, with chalk-lump walls protected by thatch, remind us that this ancient landscape has always been given over to agriculture from the time of the Stone Age farmers and herdsmen.

loneliness and desolation of some parts of this scene are pointed up by the village of Imber, which the army has taken over and half destroyed.

Wiltshire is a county of great houses below the chalk hills Longleat, with its lions, Lacock Abbey and Stourhead. The gardens of Stourhead are the most magnificent of all landscape gardens in England. They lie not far from the old stone town of Mere, close to open downland and wooded hills. Coming along the road dividing Cranborne Chase and Salisbury Plain, from the severe beauty of Wilton House and Salisbury Cathedral, you emerge at Stourhead into a perfect 'artificial' landscape.

The gardens were designed by the banker Henry Hoare between 1740 and 1760. His aim was to create in an actual garden the scenery painted by Claude and the French landscape artists. Hoare planted a valley with trees, dammed a stream to make the lakes and built temples and a grotto. The first temple, built in 1745, is of pink Chilmark stone, coloured by lichen. The Sun Temple is a

copy of one at Baalbek. The gardens were planted with azaleas and rhododendrons in the nineteenth century, and today the property belongs to the National Trust.

Stourhead is brilliant with the blossoms of such shrubs in spring, but autumn is perhaps the best time to walk in this superbly contoured and 'civilized' landscape. The vivid reds and golds of the turning trees stand high above the blue of the lakes with paths winding into further woods beyond the warm stone of the Temple of Flora. Here, by the tall weeping ash and willow trees, the tulip tree of 1750, the great fir tree with its trunk a delicate oyster-shell colour where branches have been cut off, you can pause and become a character in this 'picture' landscape. It takes over two hours to walk through the entire painting, but you seem to hold in your mind a total, poetic, almost faery landscape and to deceive yourself into thinking that these waters, these trees, beeches, firs and oaks have been settled by nature rather than by man.

Typical of many smaller pockets of downland between the sea and higher hills is St Breock Downs in Cornwall. Lying beyond the town of Wadebridge, these low rounded fields of bracken are spread about with neolithic stones, such as Maen Gurter, the Great Stone. In recent years large patches of bracken have been poisoned off, the thin soil over granite sown down to grass for sheep.

In sheltered parts of these downs thin lichen-covered trees grow in woodlands where the stonechat nests. For the rest there is nothing but space divided here and there by farmhouses, square, solid, of grey granite blocks. On both sides of the peninsula the views are magnificent, with the English Channel to the south beyond the white spoil heaps of the china clay mines round St Austell, and to the north the Bristol Channel. Here you are standing between the very low land of Cornwall, the coast, and the very high, Bodmin Moor. Buzzards use the electricity wires as hunting lodges, the fox runs down into wooded valleys. The fields are divided by narrow stone-hedged lanes, full of flowers of every kind in spring and summer, and by small hidden streams where the heron slowly manoeuvres his large wings between the trees.

Hills

A hill landscape must take in the lowlands from which it springs. In summer it is green and pastoral with a few sheep, perhaps going down a grassy track. It is a landscape such as that of Stiperstones ridge on the Welsh border of Shropshire, where nothing intervenes between the ridge and the neighbouring bracken-clad hills but two houses hidden by trees. It is the kind of landscape that denies the often-repeated statement that 'Britain is almost completely built over'. For it may well be possible to cultivate higher and higher up the slopes, but it is rarely possible to deface it with buildings.

Somerset is a county full of hill ranges – the Mendip and Quantock Hills and Exmoor. The south-west face of the Mendip Hills falls to the lowlands drained by the river Axe. These hills form a gently swelling plateau, only 1,068 feet at their highest point at Black Down, and consisting mainly of carboniferous limestone. The most famous 'scars' in this limestone occur at Cheddar Gorge and Wookey Hole. The caves at Cheddar are now little more than a floodlit tourist attraction. The gorge, however, is a miraculous piece of landscaping, the tall limestone cliffs rising each side of the road for the best part of a mile, covered in scrub and the rare Cheddar pink. Another gorge, nothing like so spectacular as Cheddar, at Burrington Coombe, has an inscription on one of its rocks announcing that in 1762 the Rev. Augustus Toplady was caught here in a storm and while sheltering conceived the hymn 'Rock of Ages'.

One might expect to find that Cheddar cheeses are being made here in local farmhouses. They still are in small quantities. But for the most part horticulture, especially strawberry growing, is the main 'industry', alongside limestone quarrying. This limestone, which forms the Mendip Hills and the Cotswolds, is capable of cracking dramatically. These cracks sometimes widen into hidden underground caverns, such as those at Cheddar and Gaping Ghyll in Yorkshire. They form underground landscapes of caves and watercourses, linked to the upper ground by funnels into which streams often disappear.

The ash tree thrives on carboniferous limestone and great stands of them beautify the Mendip Hills as they do the Derbyshire dales. The most characteristic of these Mendip ash woods is at Shapwick Heath, now a nature reserve, and there is another at Rodney Stoke on the south side of the hills.

Rock roses, lady's fingers, horse-shoe vetch, purple milk vetch, bird's foot trefoil and clover are to be found here as well as the Cheddar pink. Amongst the rarer plants growing in the Mendip limestone are spiked speedwell, rock pepperwort and, in the Avon Gorge, round-headed leek, a member of the garlic family.

The Quantock Hills, which run almost to the sea at Watchet, are bordered to the west by the Brendon Hills, and to the south by the Black Down Hills. This ridge of hills, about twelve miles long, is covered in heather, whortleberries and bracken, and there are fine sea views along the walker's track on the top. Wild deer roam here, introduced from Exmoor around 1861. In the more remote parts of the hills live badgers and foxes. Buzzard and kestrels, meadow pipits, green and spotted woodpeckers hunt in the deeply wooded coombs which are a typical feature of this landscape.

North of these gentle Quantock Hills are the Cotswolds and Chilterns. They form a kind of U-shape, with the Whitehorse Hills below.

The predominant colour of the Cotswolds is a honey-brown, seen in all the old houses in such towns as Burford. Yet when the stone is first quarried it is almost white, and only mellows with time. Furthermore, the stone itself, like some Cornish granite, has an interior luminosity which makes it glow. The roofs of the houses are covered with stone tiles (here again, like Cornwall, with its Delabole slate), which reflect the sun amongst the greens of moss, the yellows of lichens and the greys of house leeks.

The Chilterns, near West
Wycombe, Buckinghamshire
We are looking down on a
Puginesque village school
embowered in the beeches
and bathed in the opalescent
light inevitably associated
with the Chilterns. Unlike
the chalk downs of Kent,
Surrey and Sussex, Berkshire
and Wiltshire, the Chilterns
(never referred to as
'downs'), although formed
during the same Cretaceous
period, when much of the
country was submerged in a
clear sea, rise in a high scarp.
Its relation to the
direction of the ice sheets
which later passed over it
preverved it from the
planing action that shaped
the chalk downs and wolds.
The beech woods of the
Chilterns, like those in
neighbouring parts of
Oxfordshire and Berkshire
and those of the North and
South Downs, are the
descendants of ancient
forests. Beeches outside these
regions have nearly always
been planted, often as part of
18th-century landscaping.

Holywell Downs near Stow-on-the-Wold, Gloucestershire

The point of the photograph is the intense drama of the light, recorded just before the outbreak of a summer storm. The gentle landscape (a hedged instead of a walled area of the Cotswolds, with a great sense of space and skies) is electrified, and the ever-present harmony in this favoured region between man and nature is proclaimed in the boldest accents. The little farmhouse and its out-houses are built of limestone from the ground on which they stand. Even the lichen-patterned roof slates are of Cotswold stone.

The colours in the dry-stone walling of the Cotswolds range from palest grey to apricot. The actual stones which form the walls are of differing sizes, some several inches thick, others as thin as a roofing slate, depending on the quarry from which they have been taken. These hedge walls are wedge-shaped in section. Through-stones are put in to act not only as joins but as steps into and out of a field. The tops are finished off with 'cock-ups', large stones set on edge to give a serrated effect.

These hills and valleys, beginning as no more than lowlands north and west of Oxford, eventually cover the whole of Gloucestershire and wend off into Worcestershire. Chipping Norton, one of the old Cotswold wool towns, is the highest town in these Oxfordshire hills, which roll away above their quiet trout streams, the Evenlode, the Coln and the Windrush. In early June the air is full of mayfly. Along their banks grow mimulus or 'monkey flower'. In the woods I have found herb paris, wild lily-of-the-valley and figwort.

One of the most beautiful Cotswold villages is Chedworth, a stone village set round a small stream flowing to the river Coln. Here, near Yanworth, in six acres of woods, are the extensive remains of a Roman villa, with mosaic pavements and bath-house. Coming from tourist-haunted Bourton-on-the-Water or Stow-on-the-Wold, the villa in its quiet surroundings presents a dramatic con-

trast. It is a survival of life in England under the Roman occupation, but you have the impression that very little in the deep countryside has changed.

The Chilterns, clothed with beech woods, to the north of Buckinghamshire, form a steep escarpment above the Vale of Aylesbury. In the heart of these hills Bledlow Ridge is reached by a steep climb, at the foot of which is the Icknield Way. As well as beeches, cherries grow here, and that lovely tree the hornbeam. The lanes are lined with yew and oak, so characteristic of Chiltern hill country. The poet Gray summed up this landscape at Stoke Poges in his 'Elegy in a Country Churchyard':

Beneath those rugged elms, that yew tree shade,
Where heaves the turf in many a mould'ring heap,
Each in his narrow cell for ever laid,
The rude forefathers of the hamlet sleep.

Only today, of course, we no longer see the ploughman, with whom Gray opens his poem, plodding his weary way home; he drives through the lanes on a tractor. These streamless valleys are the habitat of juniper and spindle. Although many of the wild flowers which used to be found here are gone, it is

Uley, Gloucestershire
This western fringe of the Cotswold limestone scarp, with its high wild hills, hanging woods and pear orchards, presents a very different picture from the better-known landscape in the neighbourhood of Cirencester, divided after enclosure into large stone-walled fields. An extraordinary sense of antiquity and mystery pervades this stretch of the escarpment. Like so many of the landscapes of hills and downs it was neolithic country, a country of long-barrow burials, among them, close to the scene of the photograph, the delightfully named Hetty Pegler's Tump.

still possible, on some remote and unvisited grassy bank, to find a single root of golden saxifrage and the man orchid and military orchid. But if you do, it is as well to keep quiet about it.

The historic palace at Stowe is one of the glories of Buckinghamshire. A noble Corinthian arch spans an avenue of elms and beeches leading into a park of 800 acres, laid out by William Kent and 'Capability' Brown. The magnificent front of the mansion is 900 feet long. Once the seat of the Dukes of Buckingham and Chandos, it is now a public school. It stands like a small town in its 'landscape' parkland, its ornamental temples purposely leading the eye into its garden wildernesses.

The Malvern Hills rise from the valley of the river Severn to the Worcestershire Beacon, 1,395 feet high. A trench running along the summit of the hills is an ancient boundary line which still forms the county boundary. There is a wonderful panoramic view south from the top of Bredon Hill, westwards across the M5, over fifteen miles of the Malvern Plain through which runs the river Avon, across Brockeridge Common, to the Malvern Hills.

This range of pre-Cambrian rock – only nine miles long – is millions of years old. To reach this ridge you climb up through what was once a royal deer park, through commons covered in bracken and furze until you arrive at naked rocks. Go south from the Worcestershire Beacon along a tremendous saddleback until you come to 'British Camp', an Iron Age camp of about 44 acres. It has a citadel with trenches and parapets of thick stone walling.

Above Litton, Derbyshire
The most conspicuous feature of this limestone plateau is the gleaming network of silvery dry-stone walls in which the landscape is enmeshed. They date for the most part from the 18th-century Enclosure Acts.

Opposite The Herefordshire Beacon, Herefordshire
The abrupt ramparts of the Malvern Hills, rising so dramatically above the flat plains of Worcestershire and the lowlands of Hereford-shire, express the reality of geological violence with a startling sense of immediacy. The spine of archaean gneiss was thrust through the earth's crust by a gigantic upheaval at the end of the Carboniferous period. A great Iron Age fort fills the foreground of the picture; the central and highest part later became the site of a medieval castle.

79

Perhaps it was here that Langland, the Malvern-born poet, was sitting when he began that early English poem *Piers Plowman*, 'In a somer seson whan soft was the sonne.' Sitting on some shreds of shepherd's clothing he had his marvellous dream in which he saw in the valley below 'a fair field full of folk'.

The landscape on which we look down is one of rivers, meadows and orchards of damsons, apples and cherries. Hereford cattle graze the watermeadows of the river Teme beneath stands of cricket-bat willows. The view is dotted with old, half-timbered farmhouses their hop-yards, in a landscape that appears to be washed clean every morning. Even the rarer plants, such as twayblade, the butterfly orchid, the adder's tongue fern and delicate moonwort – if you can find them in the woods round Shelsley Walsh – seem freshly planted each day. And set squarely on the land, a token of a thousand harvests past, is the tithe barn at Bredon. Now owned by the National Trust, the barn is 132 feet long, and built of fifteenth-century stone.

The Long Mynd, fifteen miles south of Shrewsbury, may be described as either hill or moorland, but it provides fine walking country. If you stand above Carding Mill and turn north-east, you look into a landscape half closed in by low cloud, and crossed for the length of its heather-coloured summit by a track called the Port Way. When the cloud lifts, you can see to the Black Mountains across the border. But it can be a bleak landscape, and here amongst its hills is one of the highest golf links in England.

I am not sure whether the Cheviots, a range of thirty-five miles of border between England and Scotland, are hills or mountains. They are called hills but the Cheviot itself, the highest of the range, is 2,676 feet. They are, nevertheless, a fine group of conical, high-arched forms and except at the very top are grass-covered. Their sides are scored with narrow glens which carry the headwaters of the Till, the Coquet and North Tyne rivers on the south, with tributaries of the Tweed on the north.

In the past these hills were the scene of much border dispute and bloodshed, made famous in the ballad 'Chevy Chase'. Amidst this magnificent scenery rise the bald domes of the hills. Grasses on the slopes change colour under the wind, sun and cloud, riding across the border like massive waves. These hills form the northern third of the Northumberland National Park, of which the southern boundary is Hadrian's Wall. Looking at them from cattle-filled valleys, they appear gentle and sedate, but they can be lonely and dangerous in bad weather. The few hill farmers who live here, in houses built of whinstone rubble, a hard, intractable stone, are thin on the ground. In the hill-heather live grouse and black game and the blue mountain hare, which in winter turns white.

From the eastern end of the Cheviots, on a fine day, the landscape stretches out before you over the sea to the Farne Islands, ten miles from Berwick-upon-Tweed. These tall black basalt rocks, now a bird sanctuary managed by the National Trust, are the breeding-place of eider duck, guillemot, puffin, fulmar and petrel as well as seals.

The Cheviot Hills from Yeavering, Northumberland The Cheviot Hills are of much the same age and formation as the Pentland Hills and are of volcanic origin. Even from this distance some of the shapes of the forts and barrows can be descried, making these silent hills a prehistoric empire. Not far from this spot too, aerial photographs have revealed the site in an arable field of the 7th-century palace of Edwin of Northumbria. The heron, bird of fen and marshland, haunts these uplands, at one with their ancient spirit. Scott said of this landscape: 'The Cheviots were before me in frowning majesty; not indeed with the sublime majesty of rock and cliff which characterises mountains of the primary class, but huge, round-headed and clothed with a dark robe of russet, gaining by their extent and desolate appearance an influence upon the imagination, as a desert district possessing a character of its own.' Broom flowers in the foreground of the picture, star saxifrage and spring gentians grow in the far valley.

Right The Pentland Hills, Midlothian
Only a lowland by comparison with the great mountain masses of the Highlands, this smiling landscape of the Pentlands, 'the hills of home', as R. L. Stevenson called them because of their nearness to Edinburgh, is composed of a core of Silurian rocks with fringing outcrops of Old Red Sandstone. That is the geological picture. Coleridge spoke of the bald pates of these hills, but the scene, though powerfully sculptural, is now well wooded, conspicuously peaceful, pastoral and agricultural. Nevertheless its past was one of forays, raids and invasions from the time of the Picts to the days of the Covenanters. The hills formed one of the great barriers between the North and the South, penetrated by no more than a drove road. The scene shown here is that of Alan Ramsay's charming pastoral play *The Gentle Shepherd*, revived in recent years at the Edinburgh Festival.

Not far from the town of Melrose is Abbotsford, in its green valley, the home of Sir Walter Scott, who bought the estate and built the house in 1811. Many of the trees he planted are still standing. It is a superb position for a house amongst the Lammermuir Hills, the Moorfoots and Ettrick Forest. And only a mile from Melrose, are the Eildons, three volcanic hills where the Faery Queen is supposed to have her kingdom.

Opposite Approaching Housesteads, Hadrian's Wall, Northumberland

5 Middle Landscapes

IF you stand on the top of a church tower in, say, Lincolnshire, Huntingdonshire or Warwickshire and look over the landscape, it resembles nothing so much as one vast series of tennis courts, some green, others brown, where the land under plough has not yet yielded a crop, or golden in the aftermath of harvest. The predominant feature of the Shires is flatness. Here everything is typical of what is called 'the true English landscape'. The odd thing is that it is not dull.

These middle English landscapes are confined between the glorious colours of the Lincolnshire bulb fields in spring and the brown grass of Offa's Dyke, between the heights of the Peak District and the silvan peace of the upper Thames.

On the border between southern Herefordshire and Wales are the Black Mountains. Their landscape frowns down on the flatness, smudged with white-washed or red-stone farmhouses, while the Gospel Pass, from Llanthony Abbey to the town of Hay, emerges upon a spectacular 'vision' of the ranges of the Radnor Forest mountains, right up to Snowdon and her sister heights, Carnedd Llywelyn and Carnedd Dafydd. These mountains rise like enormous stairs above the valley treetops.

Set in this pastoral belt between the Black Mountains and the sea off Lincolnshire is the creeping, fermenting landscape of industrialization, which had its origins at Ironbridge and the Potteries. It is inescapable. Queen of this industrial region is the city of Birmingham, from which great new roads lead in all directions, splitting the landscape, creating new landscapes on the motorways, the M5 to London and the North, the A45 to Coventry and the car-industry complex, and the A38 to the beer of Burton upon Trent.

Industrialization is a ball of fire at the centre of a wonderful pastoral landscape which circles its perimeter, a landscape completely undramatic, completely traditional. Through the Vale of Evesham runs the river Avon below the Forest of Arden, where willows and other trees are reflected in its waters. With lawns here and there it meanders placidly along to join the river Severn above Gloucester. Even the kingfishers which nest and hunt in these waters seem to fly more slowly; the wagtails alight with more dignity on the small sandy islands; and the warblers sing more sweetly from its bank sedges.

In this flat, almost featureless vale are grown some of the best market-garden crops in England, certainly the best asparagus, and all salad crops, such as lettuce, radish, spring onion, to say nothing of the sprouts, cabbages, peas

Opposite Wood anemones, field poppies, wild rose and hemlock, and primroses in flower

Overleaf View from Croft Ambrey, Herefordshire This calm and lordly view from the ramparts of an Iron Age fort embraces a stretch of Old Red Sandstone soils which today makes fertile farming country and still, on the higher slopes, supports reminders of the extensive forests of pre-historic times, as well as woods planted by the Forestry Commission. The fort was later occupied by refugees from Caesar's campaigns, some of them followers of Caractacus, who was defeated to the west in the Welsh hills in AD 50. The field pattern, though typical of the English scene, is not that of the 18th- and 19th-century enclosures: Leland observed in Henry VIII's time that a great deal of land in the Welsh border countries had been reclaimed from the forest and enclosed into hedged fields. It was the abundance of pasture which made this possible. Where there was a shortage of pasture, the right to graze animals in the communally held open fields was not readily relinquished.

The Teme Valley,
Worcestershire
This vivid orchard landscape
kindles a sense of well-being,
prosperity and graciousness.
The luxuriance is all the
more striking to the
imagination by contrast
with the prevailing redness
of the soil, interpreted by
some geologists as the
product of ancient deserts.
The blossoming trees are
cherry, damson and apple,
and the photograph shows
how the orchards
characteristically alternate
with meadows. Apples have
been eaten in this district
for at least 4,000 years: seeds
of the fruits have been found
among the remains of
neolithic men. On the
slopes grow the strange
green-flowered twayblade
and the spurred white
butterfly orchid, and near
this place the photographer
found the rare and fragile
moonwort fern.

and runner beans. Just as in April it is the blossom of Pershore plum trees, the fields of daffodils and narcissi that light up this landscape, so, in high summer, the predominant colour is the crimson of runner-bean blossom, growing low to the ground or up canes and sticks. In every cottage garden in Britain the crimson of the runner bean is the colour that gives meaning to any village landscape. Stocks, pansies, roses, yes; but for me it is the crimson of the beans which astonishes.

In August plum-picking begins – the yellow egg-plum, the Prolifics, purple Pershores and, best of all, the Victorias. Almost before this harvest is over, the colour of gardens and orchards changes to a light green as the Brussels sprouts and other brassicas come on, in the fields about Bretforton, for example. This village lies on three tributaries of the river Avon and possesses a large collection of dovecots, one built by the monks of Evesham before the Dissolution of the Monasteries, and some in the seventeenth and eighteenth centuries. There is also a fine tithe barn. In agriculture and colour of land Evesham, with its fertile black soil, reflects the Fens on the other side of this middle circle of England.

To the north-west of the Vale of Evesham is that other fruit-growing district, the Teme valley, noted for its cherry orchards, pastures, hayfields and hop-yards. This is a landscape of red earth (the river Teme itself often runs red due to erosion of the sandstone soil), adorned with Hereford cattle and half-timbered farmhouses. It is a graceful landscape, in which wild flowers, such as purple loosestrife and yellow skull-cap, decorate the streams, where some of the water-meadows still grow a crop of tall, slender, cricket-bat willows, a variety of the white willow.

As you come to that great turn on the M5 at Strasham, Bredon Hill faces you, crowned by its Iron Age camp built at the end of the last century BC. Within the confines of the fort is an eighteenth-century folly, a tower known locally as Parson's Folly. There is a wonderful view over the Malvern Plain from the folly, and below the hill the Avon meanders slowly through meadows and fields.

Continuing the outer circle about the iron heart of the Midlands, the Shropshire landscape is different from that of the south-west. The river Severn still runs in its low fields and divides this county, its western boundary being the border between England and Wales, but it is a landscape of contrasts, uplands, rock formations like the Stiperstones, 'mountains' such as The Wrekin in the west, and in the north rich dairy farming and arable.

At Overton, for example, two miles out of Ludlow, you can see a complete English landscape, with all its traditional features. Everywhere you look there are stately trees, beech, oak and fir. Cattle are lowing this early September morning; the sun rises above a slight valley mist and a train passes. Your eyes are led from the yellow of harvested cornfields to the woods hanging on the opposite slopes, and then up again to Cleehill, a long sloping crag, with the radar station gleaming on its summit.

In contrast, at the sharp and bare Stiperstones you might be in Cornwall on

The Potteries, Staffordshire
The brilliance of the day, the
smoke veiling the distant
Potteries and the symmetry
of the coal tip against the
spectacular sky disguise the
devastation of this vast
landscape, accomplished in
the 18th and 19th centuries.
A tradition of pot-making in
the Five Towns goes back to
the 14th century, but the
massive development only
took place after 1800.

Rough Tor or Brown Willy, with the same broken stones leading to the summit,
the same long views over square green fields leading into a blue distant landscape, the same ravens and kestrels circling the top. The comparison goes
further in that on the western slopes of these rocks are to be found little villages,
such as Snailbeach, Perkins Beach, Shelve and The Bog, which were once lead-
mining centres and where, as in the south-west of England, there are derelict
winding houses, and traces of pits and tramways. This early industrial landscape is deserted, grown over and become a museum piece.

The long view of landscape is seen once more from the limestone scarp,
Wenlock Edge, wooded for much of its twelve miles. From its top you can
almost look down into Ironbridge Gorge on the river Severn. Spanning the

stream is the iron bridge itself, the precursor of the industrial landscapes in the heart of this middle region of England. Here in the Shropshire coalfield Abraham Darby first smelted iron with coke and in 1779 his grandson built the bridge. From one side of the bridge you look down at the villages on the steep slopes of the gorge, from the other into woods with the Severn running between. Once this peaceful landscape was filled with the light of blast furnaces and the din of forge hammers. Silvan and green, proto-industrial, Ironbridge preserves the early years before the mammoth towns of today took shape, destroying old landscapes and creating modern ones. A little down stream stand the creeper-covered ruins of Bedlam Furnace. The artist Cotman came here and painted the scene in 1802. Turner, attracted by the 'hellish light' from the furnaces, painted 'Lime Kiln at Coalbrookdale' about 1797.

In the north-west of Shropshire is that curious region known locally as 'The Lake District', a series of small lakes clustering about the town of Ellesmere and the Llangollen Canal. The largest of these meres comes right up to the town, its waters inhabited by pike.

The little river Tern flows not far from Hodnet and the 'romantic' Hawkstone Park, both artificial landscapes which take you out of Shropshire into Leicester-shire across the M6. Hodnet has gardens of some sixty acres, built from 1922 on-wards from a wilderness of scrub in a narrow, marshy valley. Centred round a string of pools of various shapes and sizes beneath forest trees, are lawns and plantings of rhododendrons, azaleas, lilies, roses and peonies.

These gardens are in sharp contrast to Hawkstone Park, a long rocky ridge of red sandstone cliffs with isolated crags between. From the modern golf course in part of the grounds can be seen the ruins of the Red Castle and the Obelisk, built in 1795 and standing 112 feet high. The two, Hodnet and Hawkstone Park, are 'linked' by what seems, at first sight, to be another red castle on a small hill. It is, in fact, nothing but a folly.

Having come across the half circle, below the Peak District, you are on the east side of the industrial heart. The valley of the river Welland divides Rutland (now part of Leicestershire) from Northamptonshire in much the same way as the river Soar cuts Leicestershire in half as it flows to the Trent. The A6 from London to Manchester might be said to do the same.

The scenery of Northamptonshire can be very well taken in from the village of Harringworth with its fourteenth-century cross. Only the spire of the church rises above the long railway viaduct, crossing the valley over the river Welland. The landscape, from every point of view, seems to be dominated by this viaduct, which is built of a hard-glazed bluish brick. Weather, however, has left its mark by splitting off the blue outer skin of some of the bricks to reveal the red interior, so giving the impression that it was built of red and blue bricks. The arches, eighty-two of them, each numbered in the usual fashion starting from the London end, are beautifully proportioned, leaping across the water-meadows to divide the low fields from the small rising farmlands beyond. When a train crosses it the whole structure seems to be in flight southwards.

The Welland Viaduct
near Seaton, Rutland
The great brick railway
viaduct built in 1876–8
links the former county of
Rutland and Northampton-
shire across the broad levels
of the Welland valley. The
valley now, since the
dwindling and disappearance
of ancient villages, lonely
country, was settled very
early in the Saxon period,
for it was one of the most
used routes into the heart
of the midlands.

Two places remain in the memory: the landscape view from the terrace of the great avenue at Castle Ashby, riding away into the distance under deep, dark winter skies over the seven ornamental lakes in the park, and the pathetic Castle Mound at Fotheringay, where Richard III was born and Mary Queen of Scots was imprisoned and eventually executed.

Such places, with their historical associations, cast a melancholy over the landscape. They are almost too sad to contemplate. Now all that can be seen at Fotheringay is the bushy mound above a farmhouse beside the river Nene. The Queen died on 8 February 1587, her little dog hidden in her skirts. After the macabre execution – the Queen's hair was a wig and came away when the executioner tried to lift her head – the little dog refused to leave her body but 'lay between her head and her shoulders'.

As for Leicestershire, it is a landscape dominated by fox-hunters and great Shire horses. The great heartlands of iron works, power stations, blast furnaces and so on, have their counterparts in these majestic horses still found occasionally working on the farms. These heavy horses, the Shires, can be seen along with Clydesdales and Suffolk Punches, at every agricultural show in the summer in England. They are the truly 'great' animals of the countryside.

The Shire horse, which may be taller than seventeen hands, is the oldest of the heavy horses, being mentioned in a statute of Henry VII. They have about them the aura of ancient battle, when men put on that impossibly heavy armour and rode at one another with long spears, toppling each other into the dust. They retain even today this aura of chivalry, and were often referred to as the War Horse. The earth shivered and thundered as they gathered what little speed they could manage to engage the enemy.

The Clydesdale, as its name implies, comes from the valley of the Clyde in Scotland. Like the Shire horse, it is distinguished by the 'feathers', or silky hairs, on the back of the legs. The Suffolk Punch is always chestnut, and its short sturdy legs have no feathers. There is nothing more evocative of the deep countryside of one hundred years ago than to see today (and this is still possible in parts of Suffolk) a team of Punches ploughing a field with its attendant crowd of gulls and and other birds. I must have been one of the last to see that wonderful ancient custom, the dressing of the stallion before he sets out along the lanes with his 'servant', a farmhand, to serve the local mares. He would tread the road like an Emperor in his finery, his head arched, his pride manifest in every step, the complete symbol of fertility and potency.

Most landscape, as I have said, displays the work of man. The Leicestershire landscape might have been purposely laid out for fox-hunting; even the woods seem tamed, used as fox coverts. The fields in this gently rolling clay country are divided by thorn hedges, punctuated by ash trees, put in as standards. Many of these hedges date back to the Enclosure Acts of the Georgian period, when thorn was often used for it made a fast-growing hedge. Even the road hedges here are wide enough to hide a fox at its last gasp. It can be said that the colour of man in this landscape is crimson, the hunting redcoat and the blood

of his victim, 'the unspeakable in pursuit of the uneatable', as Oscar Wilde said.
I do not think that any man of sensibility who has once seen a hunted fox, or
any other wild animal, at its ending before the hounds fall on it and tear it to
pieces, could ever agree to this form of 'sport'.

Not quite all of Leicestershire is given over to the Hunts, picturesque though
they may be. North-west of Leicester is Charnwood Forest with its 212 acres of
trees and moors. At Bradgate Park and Swithland Wood there are nature
reserves. This is a landscape, once more, of granite outcrops and brackened
hills, where Lady Jane Grey spent her youth learning Latin and Greek under
her tutor, Aylmer, in the house, now a ruin, in Bradgate Park.

Another fine landscape walk, beyond the forest, is at Bardon Hill, the highest
part of Leicestershire, some 912 feet above sea-level. The 'summit' provides an
excellent look-out across the most varied of landscapes to the Malvern Hills
and The Wrekin, to the Black Mountains on one side and The Wash on the
other. On a fine day Lincoln Cathedral can be seen rising from the conglomer-
ation of factories and collieries which lie below and around it, an extraordinary spiritual symbol in the centre of a modern world.

Canals are another feature of Leicestershire. Foxton has a system of ten locks

The Vale of Catmose,
Rutland
The charm of this quiet
Midland countryside is that
it bears no mark of the
Industrial Revolution. The
high ground near the grand
mansion of Burley-on-the-
Hill on which the photo-
grapher stood is a ridge of
limestone, below which lies
the valley of Catmose, a clay
landscape formed in the
Jurassic period. Its present
appearance, like that of the
ample Warwickshire
prospect shown on page 101,
is due very largely to Parliamentary enclosure, although
the level fields of this orderly
panorama adjoin a terrain of
irregular hedged enclosures
going back to the 16th
century and earlier.

carrying those brightly painted narrow boats as well as tourist craft uphill from
the Grand Union Canal to the Market Harborough Basin. Walking along the
tow paths of these placid canals you are in a fine pastoral landscape, except
where they pass through the drabber parts of towns.

The landscape of Rutland, now absorbed into Leicestershire, is quite different.
For one thing the limestone belt, from Dorset to Yorkshire, assures us that the
buildings will be much the same as those of the Cotswolds, villages of warm
stone, massive agricultural barns, and stone walls for hedges. Although Rutland
is predominantly a farming county, ironstone is mined from open-cast work-
ings, and along the Stamford to Oakham road is a large new reservoir.

Oakham itself is a typical Rutland town, the buildings straight-lined and
clean, while Ayston, a pretty village, has ironstone cottages with roofs of thatch
or Collyweston slate. The farmhouses, cottages and church of Braunston, too,
are built of this dark-brown local ironstone. The village rises in hilly country
above the river Gwash, and nearby is the village of Upper Hambleton on its hill,
providing fine views over the Vale of Catmose.

The view north-east of Hambleton is for me the most romantic landscape in
Rutland. It contains the desolate ruins of the church at Pickworth, where the
poet Clare worked as a lime-burner and wrote his poem 'Elegy on the Ruins of
Pickworth'.

These buried ruins, now in dust forgot,
These heaps of stone the only remnants seen –
'The Old Foundations' still they call the spot
Which plainly tells inquiry what has been –

A time was once, though now the nettle grows
In triumph o'er each heap that swells the ground,
When they, in buildings pil'd, a village rose,
With here a cot, and there a garden crowned.

Such deserted villages, like the ruins of Fotheringay Castle, are the deep melancholy music of landscape without which the awe-inspiring beauty of mountains, the excitement of the seashore, the peculiar comfort of meadowland, and the exhilaration of rivers could not be complete. Over and above their archaeological interest, their historical meaning, they form the diagram of a way of life, for the landscapes we see today were seen then by the villagers who were dispossessed. Even in their ruins these deserted places are still as much theirs as ours.

At the far eastern arc of this middle landscape circle, in Lincolnshire, is one of the most unusual nature trails in the country. Gibraltar Point, near Skegness, is a sea trail over salt marshes and through sand dunes, and at the point there is a bird sanctuary. We are back in a watery landscape, the water fauna and flora

Fields near Trumpington, Cambridgeshire
This chalky landscape was probably cleared of its woodland covering during the Roman occupation. The large open fields of medieval England have survived into our own century, for this was never a region of hedges. The isolated farm nevertheless dates from the period of Parliamentary enclosure of pastures. The redistribution of the land at that time in blocks, instead of in strips scattered throughout the parish, prompted many farmers to build new farmsteads in the middle of their compact territory. Before this time, except for a few farmhouses built in isolation as a result of Tudor or Stuart enclosures, farmers lived in the village.

of the Fens. Long, sandy yellow paths lead between patches of deep-green scrub with the blue of the sea always ahead. Such trails – another is on the Elsham Hall estate, near Brigg – are vital for the preservation and appreciation of landscape and the mental refreshment that they afford.

Yet in summer it is the seascapes not the landscapes that draw the holiday-makers in their thousands. This carnival of the long months takes place in a scene of artificial structures, on immense stretches of yellow sand at Skegness, with its pier like an aerodrome runway, or at the Astroglide at Cleethorpes in brilliant red and blue, or on the donkeys at Mablethorpe. To be enjoyed everything must be thrown away until half-warm beer in ornate beer halls becomes a drink more delicious than nectar, and fish and chips, shellfish, or sticks of rock, food more precious than nightingale's tongues.

Behind the Lincoln Marsh, north of The Wash, lie the Wolds, almost isolated from heavy through-traffic. This is a little-known area of deep farming land, green in spring, golden in early autumn, full of small villages, a remote conservative landscape, by which I mean that it changes little from one century to another, except in the actual farming processes, certainly not in seed-time and harvest.

You are more likely to meet a combine-harvester or a muck-spreader than cars in these narrow lanes. The colour of this wide landscape is increased by the brilliance of the agricultural machinery, the reds of tractors, the light blue of spidery hay-tedding machines, the rich silver of a hard-worked set of ploughshares. A landscape, too, of wide skies between the river Humber and the Fens about The Wash, skies full of larks all spring and summer, which on hot days shimmer with heat-haze, creating fantastic oases of cities that do not exist. Being so close to the sea it is also a landscape filled with gulls and other sea birds. The smell of the sea is everywhere.

For me it is impossible to consider a landscape without the buildings and their history, from the delicacy of Lincoln Cathedral, say, towering over the Fens and low country, to Ludlow Castle in Shropshire. The ruined arches of Crowland Abbey, its tower and dumpy steeple set in the green lawns of its graveyard, are a fixed point for me, timelessly looking out towards that other Fenland ruin at Woodhall Spa set in magnificent pine woods, or south, across Morris Fen, to the ruins of Thorney Abbey, of which only the tall west front and nave remain. Here Hereward the Wake, that boyhood hero, made one of his last stands against William the Conqueror.

And so to the magnificence of Burghley House outside Stamford, just in Huntingdonshire. 'Capability' Brown designed the gardens with their orangery, the superb lake and bath-house, and the fine rose garden. Burghley, like Stowe, is one of the permanencies of landscape building. And coming from the ancient to modern you reach the tulip landscapes round Spalding, where vast plantations of red and yellow flowers fill the whole air with colour. How curious it is to walk in these bulb fields at dusk, when the yellow heads are like golden sovereigns nodding in the breeze, the red like spots of blood, and all of them, mixed with other colours, a shield spread upon the black earth.

Duddenhoe End, Essex
The peculiar use of the word 'End' in north-west Essex and north-east Hertfordshire points to the extensive forest ancestry of the area. As a result of individual squatting in woodland clearings villages tended to straggle, and tiny hamlets grew up away from the main settlement, giving rise to such names as North End, Paynes End, Sewards End and Duddenhoe End. The irregular hedged fields shown in this photograph were enclosed direct from the original forest during the Middle Ages. It is a landscape where there were never open fields.

The last section of this interior circle of landscape can be completed by turning directly south of Huntingdon, through the fritillary woods of Oxfordshire, which remind me always of the fritillary fields at Framsden, near Woodbridge, in Suffolk. I must agree with Geoffrey Grigson, the poet, who said that anyone living in the north or west, outside the fritillary counties, should walk at least once in a field of these flowers before he dies. Bumble bees love the plant with its mauve and white flowers, known also as the 'Snake's Head' because of its appearance. For itself, it likes best damp meadows and the edges of woods, particularly in the Thames valley and in Suffolk. But, with so much land going under the plough, it is becoming rarer. I have grown them successfully for some years beneath a hedge in my garden in Cornwall, as a reminder of these Oxfordshire spinneys and long days spent about the ruins of Godstow.

Indeed, a walk from Oxford itself, along the footpaths of Port Meadow to the Trout Inn and the ruins of the Priory at Godstow, can give one as fine a picture of the landscape as anywhere in the county. Fair Rosamunde, the mistress of Henry II, died at the Priory in 1176. Henry kept her at Woodstock, but Queen Eleanor, seeing the King one day 'with the end of a ball of floss attached to his spur', followed him and found a secret place in a thicket. While the King was away she searched this thicket and discovered a low door cunningly concealed. It led to a bower in which was a young girl 'of incomparable beauty'. She was Rosamunde Clifford, who, as a punishment, was shut up in Godstow Priory for the rest of her life.

Another impressive Oxfordshire landscape is at Goring Gap, where the Thames flows through the chalk. The Chilterns and Berkshire Downs rise at each side of the Gap, and the ancient trackway, the Icknield Way, here joins the river. The woods and hills are spectacular especially in autumn. Yet, as if to set off the industrial landscapes of Birmingham and Coventry, in the centre of this circle, here, at Cowley are the factories of one of the biggest car industries in the world, the British Leyland Corporation.

I never go into Oxfordshire without visiting that lovely village on the river Windrush, Minster Lovell, sheltered by a rising hill between Witney and Burford. After championing Lambert Simnel in the Battle of Stoke Francis Lovell returned here to a locked room, where he lay in hiding. The servant, however, who was looking after him, died suddenly in another part of the house and Lord Lovell was unable to free himself. In 1708 during restoration work on the house, a vaulted room was discovered, containing a skeleton seated at a table with the skeleton of a dog at its feet. Was it Lord Francis Lovell?

Ancient and modern landscapes coalesce in those odd, gnarled stones in their prehistoric circle, the Rollright Stones. From this ridge, surrounded by fir trees, you can look over wide views of Warwickshire. Below is the village of Little Rollright, forgotten in the serenity of its meadows and cottages.

To complete the circle, then, we have come almost into Warwickshire, into a landscape not only of great industries, but into Shakespeare country, the river Avon and those two castles Kenilworth and Warwick. Alas Kenilworth itself is

now little more than a dormitory town for the car city of Coventry. The castle yet holds in its ruined towers the mystery captured in the painting by David Cox (1804) of a fortress amongst trees, with the meadows below full of sheep. Cromwell left it in ruins, but it has been called 'the grandest fortress ruin in England'.

In Warwickshire one is always conscious of the industrial landscape in the north of the Shire at Birmingham and Coventry. At Birmingham (now almost a city of fly-overs on motorways), with over a million inhabitants, are the factories and offices of international concerns producing jewellery, toys, brass and plastic and chocolate at Bournville.

Coventry, for all its industrialization, provides the contrast of destruction and resurrection. Much of it was wiped out in the German air raids of November 1940. Photographs of the city shortly after show landscapes of despair. But look down from the air on the city today. The tall rising buildings, the glass offices, which seem to float above the immense concrete ring road, and the new cathedral, are the landscapes of hope and achievement, epitomized in the rosy sandstone with which the cathedral is built, the Graham Sutherland tapestry, the glorious interior colouring, the deep greens, purples and reds of the glass stretching from floor almost to the roof.

The countryside of Warwickshire is dominated by Shakespeare. Did he see the first Queen Elizabeth, in 1575, when she visited Leicester at Kenilworth? He was eleven then. There is still a little left of the Forest of Arden, west of Coventry, such as appears in *As You Like It*. Here in the forest is the village of Meriden, supposedly the centre of England.

Snitterfield, Warwickshire
The landscape is that of George Eliot's novels, fertile and heavy, with flat fields, massive hedgerows, well-grown elms, grazing cattle and trim farms, all steeped in the sunshine of a temperate afternoon. These fields are more precisely associated, however, with Shakespeare, for the poet's grandfather, Richard Shakespeare, farmed this land for Robert Adam. At that time it wore a rather different aspect, for unlike the fields at Duddenhoe End (page 98), these pastures are largely the creation of Georgian enclosure. When the hedges were new, the prospect must have looked bleak, but now in their maturity, the hawthorn interspersed with elm, they give the appearance in the distance of an almost continuing wood.

6 Forests, Woods and Hedges

Forests and Woods

BRITAIN has always been a landscape of trees, and five thousand years ago massive forests covered almost the whole island. Many of the original varieties have changed, but two of the most interesting of such ancient woods remain.

The first, in East Anglia, near Orford, is Staverton Forest or Thicks, an ancient wood of oak and holly, said to have been planted by the Druids, where King Edmund was martyred in 870 by the invading Danes. The hollies are enormous, huge towering boles growing beside the oaks and, in some cases, actually from their roots. The oaks are the most extraordinary of all. They must be hundreds of years old, shrunken, queer-shaped monstrosities, grotesque half-dead hollow shells of trees which were in their prime under the first Queen Elizabeth.

Beneath the entwined branches of these hollies and oaks are centuries of leaf mould, decaying year after year in the cold and silence of an east-coast winter. Fronds of holly hang down like liana in a jungle. The entire forest is alive with birds nesting or feeding on the berries. This is an Arthur Rackham forest, the skin of the hollies wrinkled and covered in warts, the holes and angles of branches green with mosses. The undergrowth of bramble, ivy, purple loose-strife, dog's mercury, and bluebells is abundant.

The other singular forest is on Dartmoor. Wistman's Wood is some way across the moor from the road at Two Bridges, and can only be visited when the Army is not using the firing range along the valley. The wood runs for 400 yards along the left bank of the West Dart river in the heart of Dartmoor Forest itself. Whereas at Staverton the oaks and hollies are massive, in Wistman's Wood the oaks are diminutive and stunted. I have actually sat on the top of one of them with my feet touching the ground. This 'bonsai' appearance is due to the granite boulders in which they are growing; the remains of a disintegrated tor, locally called 'a cluster', the loose masses of granite protect the roots. These blocks are themselves covered in green mosses. Beneath these small trees, hundreds of years old – there are more at Black Tor Copse on the left bank of the West Ockment river – the ground is covered with bramble and bilberry, ivy and the large woodrush, lichens and ferns flourishing in the moist conditions of wood and moor.

The names of the old forests are well known: Radnor, Savernake the Forest of Dean, Sherwood, Delamere and the New Forest. Very little pure medieval

In Staverton Thicks, Suffolk The tangled silhouette of an oak typifies the rare survival at Staverton of an ancient forest, where decaying oaks, descendants of the original trees, mingle with giant hollies and struggling saplings. In the 13th century, when the word *park* meant no more than 'an enclosure', usually a piece of natural woodland, the Thicks became the hunting park of the Staverton family, two of whom are commemorated by headless brasses in Eyke church. The Stavertons' old manor house stood in the forest until it burned down during a peasants' rising. The forest itself was never cleared.

Above In the Gwyllt,
Portmeirion, Merioneth
It is easy when looking at
these hoary, lurching yews,
part of an ancient headland
forest, to feel at one with
primitive man, who saw
trees as living beings with
powers of thought and will
and feelings like his own.
An overpowering sense of
strong, rooted life emanates
from these great fibrous,
fissured trunks. Like the oak
the yew lives to a great age:
a tree at Fortingall in Scotland was said to be more
than a thousand years old
and a yew at Brabourne in
Kent was traditionally
supposed to have endured
for the fantastic period of
thirty centuries.

forest is left, and what little remains has probably been interplanted with
conifers.

At the time of the Tudors Sherwood Forest must have been magnificent.
Even when it was split up into 'Dukeries' after Henry VIII dissolved the monasteries it must still have been a great forest with immense clearings to house the
aristocratic mansions at Worksop, Welbeck, Rufford and Newstead. I can
remember, when I was a boy, motoring down the long straight roads, through
alleyways of trees and past the splendid monumental gateways to the mansion
drives. I can recall the intensely green landscape, heavy with leaf and the woodland parks full of deer.

Now modern forestry methods, as at Cannock Chase, have taken over. But
remnants of woods still stand above valleys, lanes and the wide roads from one
mansion to the next as, for example, between Birklands, with its massed beech
and silver birch, and Bilhagh, with the finest remains of the old Sherwood
Forest that Robin Hood is supposed to have known so well.

Twenty million trees, oak, ash, holly and conifer, and two thousand miles of
forest paths, go to create the Forest of Dean in Gloucestershire, the oldest
forest in England, and one of our largest primeval forests. It is still possible,

but rarely, to come across a charcoal burner here. Charcoal was used extensively for smelting iron ore and is one reason for the disappearance of ancient forests in Kent and Sussex. The method was to stack the wood into heaps. These were partially covered with earth to limit the access of air, which had to be expertly controlled. The heap was fired and allowed to burn itself out. Charcoal was used in the making of gunpowder, from burnt alder wood. At one time gunpowder factories were set up in the Lake District and in the New Forest beside alder coppices. Today alder buckthorn, a non-thorny native of wet land, makes a fine charcoal for slow fuses. The twigs of spindle, a chalk-hill shrub, are said to make the finest artist's charcoal.

Beneath the Forest of Dean is a coal field of 22,000 acres, the 'tips' of which are disguised by broom and birch-scrub, tall bracken and foxgloves. The Purple Emperor butterfly used to haunt the forest rides, but now they are very scarce indeed. In April 1974 the Royal Society for the Protection of Birds established a bird reserve in 375 acres of the Nagshead Enclosure in the Forest. This reserve, mainly of oak wood planted in 1814 for the building of ships for the Royal Navy, has been made available by the Forestry Commission, who will admit visitors.

Sussex can still boast the largest collections of oaks at St Leonard's Forest. Ashdown Forest, also in Sussex, north of Uckfield, is made up of thousands of acres of heath and woodland providing wonderful walking country. The highest point of the Forest is Crowborough Beacon, 792 feet high. Oddly enough the majority of the trees are not ash, but oak, Scots pine, hazel and sweet chestnut.

One of the reasons ornithologists go to the New Forest is to observe that rare bird the Dartford warbler, whose main habitat is the gorse and heather heaths of the open parts of the forest. Originally named after the Kent town of Dartford where the bird used to breed, it is today only found (and then not often) on such large heaths. At one time, before the massive afforestation, it was also found in Breckland in East Anglia. Now its only haunts are the New Forest and certain heathlands in Dorset. The bird is dark grey above, maroon below, its song a harsh 'chack'.

Many other species of bird are to be seen in the New Forest, the commonest being the meadow pipit and linnet. That other 'rare' bird the hoopoe does come most summers and has been seen as far away as Selborne. Many varieties of deer are to be found here, too, including the Japanese Sika around Beaulieu.

The Forestry Commission, which was set up in 1919, now holds almost three millions acres of land, of which more than half carries tree crops. It is almost impossible to go anywhere in Britain without seeing huge masses of these dark, impenetrable woods. When you are driving towards this type of forest country the wide stands of trees look like splashes of deep green in a child's painting, wedges of colour brushed on to the surrounding fields and open countryside.

The general range of planting is Sitka spruce, Douglas fir, western hemlock, silver fir, western red cedar and lodge-pole pine, though the present policy of

Opposite Oaks at Croft, Herefordshire
The oak, with its firm, massive knobbly trunk and twisting, spreading branches, is the most famous tree of the English woodland and it has played a great part in our history. All our ships were once built of it and the giants of former forests are preserved in the timbers and panelling of medieval and Elizabethan houses and the carved roofs of churches. The wood is strong and durable and grows harder with the years. Pliny gave the age of the veteran oak as 2,000 years and scientists have established that the age of 1,200 years has occasionally been surpassed. These Croft oaks were described in a guide of 1808 as 'large and majestic exceeding in dimension those that grow in any other part of the kingdom'. The one in the foreground of the photograph has a girth of 40 ft.

The oak was sacred in pre-Christian Britain and, like the Druidical mistletoe which grows on it, was held to be a protection against fire and lightning. In remote country places people still believe an oak gives safety in a storm. The acorn at the end of the cord on old-fashioned spring blinds originated as a charm against lightning.

Winter in the Forest of Dean, Gloucestershire
The photograph was taken on a windless, lead-grey winter day without sun, when mist blurred the distant network of twigs, but when every nearby branch was sharply outlined by snow. The silence was absolute. The forest lies between the Severn and the Wye and its immensely varied terrain includes much comparatively open country, old-established villages, very few level stretches and striking contrasts between high ridges and deep valleys. The mixed trees described in the text of this book grow on a series of Old Red Sandstone, limestone and carboniferous rock. The oaks of the forest provided the timber for ships long before the reserve for this purpose was planted in 1814. It was because of the special association of the Forest of Dean with ship-building that the Spaniards were instructed in the 16th century to destroy it before anything else in Britain.

Leaving the path for an overgrown declivity to the right, the ground was strewn with rotting trunks, speckled with rubbery or spongy fungus, sheathed in dark-green moss, falling into dust. The forest has always been attractive as a source of minerals; charcoal burning and iron mining were practised from pre-historic times to the end of the Second World War. Coal mining has been going on sporadically throughout the centuries and large Roman slag heaps are still conspicuous in the under-growth.

the Commission leans more to a mixture of the above with broad-leaved, deciduous trees.

These forests have completely changed the landscape of Britain since the end of the Great War, yet the Commission is really doing no more than the large landowners of the past, though in a different way. Thomas Johnes, for example, came to Hafod, near Ysbyty Ystwyth in Cardiganshire in 1783. Here he began to plant up all the wild hills of his estate, not only because he was interested in forests, but to better the condition of the poor workers in the district. In 1801 he could write: 'My plantations are generally made on such land as I cannot plough. I plant the sides of the mountains which are universally composed of argillaceous shisters on slate rock, the surface of which is decomposed by exposure to the atmosphere and admits the roots of trees to penetrate therein and grow luxuriantly.'

Johnes planted nearly three million trees, of which over a million were larches. Two World Wars, alas, accounted for the felling of most of his plantings, and what was once his estate, visited by many celebrated people while he was alive, is now part of the Forestry Commission's Ystwyth Forest.

Where mountain sides are concerned you have only to go to the Dovey Forest at Dinas-Mawddwy in Merioneth to see the curious transformation which can be made by these Commission plantings. Here are two high hills, one clothed with the green of fir trees, the other, just across a small valley, almost as bald as when George Borrow walked here. The contrast is exhilarating.

One of the most awe-inspiring 'new' forests is down the Rheidol Gorge, cutting deeply into the hills above Devil's Bridge, near Hafod. Not far away is some of the grandest landscape and scenery in Wales. The Uwchygarreg by-road is a mile and a half out of the town of Machynlleth. It is best to walk this road, which comes down into the remote gorge of the Afon Hengwm, until it climbs through spruce woods to a long slope, where there are wonderful views of waterfalls and sheer crags before the road emerges on to a plateau of sheep walks running south to Plynlimon Pass.

At Coed-y-brenin Forest in Merioneth the Commission has interplanted conifers with broad-leaved woodlands. The new plantations are skilfully blended in with the fields, forming deep green shadows on each side of the valley. They form a healthy landscape, in balance within itself and with its surroundings.

When the first plantings of these huge forests began, the outcry against them was almost as great as that against the creation of reservoirs today. They were too symmetrical, it was said, and they destroyed the natural habitats of birds and flowers. Now, over fifty years later, many of these forests are mature, their austerity has been softened and their beauty can be seen.

The difference between the old and new forests can clearly be seen by comparing the old plantation of beech in Slindon Park, West Sussex, with a plantation of conifers in Park Hill Enclosure in the Forest of Dean. Both types of tree are tall and straight; both have leaf canopies that almost exclude the sky. But the ground beneath the beech forest is a mat of leaves; beneath the

Above Thetford Chase, Norfolk; *right* Breckland pines near Cockley Cley, Norfolk
The two contrasting landscapes belong to the same strongly individual region of light, sandy soil on the border of Norfolk and Suffolk known as Breckland. One of these landscapes is man-made, while the other exhibits the character of the original heath. One, the work of the Forestry Commission, is made up of dusky, alien monotonous ranks of Scots and Corsican pines, the other is enlivened by single wind-shaped pines.

Douglas fir of the Forest of Dean there is nothing except, at the edge of the rides, a fine covering of bracken.

In Wales and Scotland it is the mountains that help to soften the sameness of these modern forests, but in East Anglia, for the most part, this is not so. In the Brecklands, that area of sand and heath about the towns of Brandon and Thetford, the huge state forests of over 50,000 acres of Scots and Corsican pine are walls intruding on the open beauty of the heath. Climb to the top of one of the fire-watchtowers and survey the endless expanse of dark and light green trees below you. You might think yourself in Austria. In winter, under snow, this effect is more marked still.

If you penetrate these forests, coming down the wide rides to an occasional small meadow, you emerge with a feeling of escaping from the prison of a lifeless world. It is not, of course, quite true to say that no birds or flowers inhabit these planned forests, though very few can. I have walked through the rides of such forests on Dartmoor on Christmas Day, when the ice-covered

Forests, Woods and Hedges

Cod Wood, Boyland, Devon. The wood of sycamore, holly, ash, oak and elm, buoyantly fresh and newly leaved, clothes the rich valley of the Teign below broad, rounded hills which are typically bare of trees and which are geologically of the same formation as Dartmoor (see page 177). The sycamores are not indigenous: they were only introduced into England during the last quarter of the 16th century. The contrast between the wooded valley and the bleak upland is one of the pleasures of this stretch of country near Moretonhampstead. The wood itself, though it looks so mild, conceals cruel masses of granite which seem only to be prevented from crashing down to the water by thick chains of ivy. In the time of Henry II Cod Wood was a preserve of Drogo de Teign, after whom the grim castle built by Lutyens at the head of the river gorge is named.

green verges made a sound like crushed glass, and listened to the soft whisperings of goldcrests feeding high in the fir branches, a blackbird turning over dead leaves and pine needles for food, and the 'yaffle' of a green woodpecker. In Cornwall, where the old aerodrome at Davidstow is planted with firs, I have heard thrushes and blackbirds singing but have never found the nest of any bird. Little can live – or wish to live – in the dark, stygian interior of these endless lines of straight trees. Of course, deer and cattle, sheep and small rodents do come into the trees, not only because the width of the concrete runways allows them passage from one side of the moor to the other, but because the wide grass verges, where a few wild flowers do flourish, are good cropping. These verges in most forests support the broad buckler fern, the male fern and, in the deep shade, certain fungi.

The profound silence of these vast gatherings of trees is their strangest characteristic. The food-chain does not develop here is in the old native forests. This food-chain is a simple process. Trees and plants provide the food for most other organisms which are then fed on by other organisms. It is really the old rhyme: 'Great fleas have little fleas upon their backs to bite 'em, and little fleas have lesser fleas, and so *ad infinitum*'. Only with this new type of conifer forest there is no longer any *infinitum*. The end of this particular food-chain is now.

Yet how magnificent it is, and almost spine-chilling, to be in a wide ride of one of these mature forests, when a gale is blowing. The intense soughing of the treetops creates a sound which, in winter or summer, gives one the very idea of what Siberia must be like. Only the wolves are missing!

It is a relief, nevertheless, to turn from these man-made forests, acknowledging the expertise of the foresters who create and maintain them, to the small woodlands, many of which still exist as parts of vanished estates, or as remnants of older royal forests.

The summer oak woods, ripened in leaf to twice their springtime size, stand majestically over the scene at Euston in Suffolk, home of the Duke of Grafton. The roads and rivers are canopied over by them. The open spaces and lawns seem to await the start of some long-forgotten Elizabethan masque. But these forests too are the work of man and many of these trees were planted by the diarist John Evelyn. They display a sophisticated approach to nature and seem to hold their position because an artist willed it so.

Another small wood, beyond the village of Staplehurst in Kent, is full of oak, ash and elm, bordered by avenues of massive rhododendrons of every possible colour and alive with birds of all kinds. Hay Wood, on the outskirts of Wadebridge in Cornwall, is the habitat of herons, which fish the tiny streams, while many kinds of small bird nest in the lichened trees. Parts of this wood have been taken over by the Forestry Commission and planted up, but in their small beginnings the conifers cannot destroy the bracken and wild flowers. At certain times of the year the entire woodland is carpeted bright red with campion and purple loosestrife, or blue with bluebells. In Autumn the russet of dying blackberry bushes make the woodland rides look as if hung with velvet.

In a very real sense such small woods are the essence of what the old forests were like before they were felled to build ships under the Tudors, or to burn up into charcoal to smelt iron ore and, in this century, by the demands of the last two wars. When men first began to settle the land the forests were full of hazel coppices and chestnut plantations. Later hazel was used in the wattle and daub houses in East Anglia and today is used for making hurdles for sheep-folds. There are still chestnut plantations near Ashridge in Hertfordshire, and coppices in Sussex from which chestnut paling is made and the cleft oak and chestnut fencing used for paddocks.

Of all woodland trees my favourite is the hornbeam, one of Britain's most ancient trees. It is worth going into Epping Forest (or what is left of it) to look at the hornbeams, for they may not be there much longer. Nearby at Loughton the hornbeams stand in close formation, their feet in a carpet of brown autumn leaves. John Evelyn wrote of the hornbeam in his book *Silva, or a Discourse on Forest Trees* (1662), one of the earliest attempts at conservation, written 'to prevent the sensible and notorious decay of our Wooden Walls': 'it makes good yoke-timber and heads of beatles [wooden mallets], stocks and handles of tools are made from it. It makes good fire-wood, where it burns like a candle.'

No picture of England's forests and woods would be complete without a glance at the beech woods and the flora and fauna they shelter. These beautiful trees dominate the escarpments of the Chilterns and all the downs of the southern counties, as at Selborne in Hampshire, where Gilbert White lived and wrote his *Natural History of Selborne* in 1789. The National Trust now owns 240 acres of the common and parts of the hanging beech woods overlooking Selborne stream on the long and short 'lythes'.

The most majestic beech wood, some 2,300 acres in size, is Savernake Forest in Wiltshire, which dates from before the Norman Conquest. Many of the splendid beech avenues, however, were planted in the eighteenth century. The Grand Avenue, running north-west to south-east is, perhaps, the most wonderful of all beech avenues in England. The forest is well known, too, for its varieties of fungi, and deer roam among the trees.

So thick is the canopy of leaves in most beech plantations that hardly any plants grow beneath the trees, which stand, winter and summer, majestic in height and colouring. Two plants that do thrive here are white helleborine and cuckoo pint. You may even be lucky enough to find yellow bird's nest and bird's nest orchid. Near the edges of such woods one of the loveliest of all wild flowers, enchanter's nightshade, can be found in spring. Small, elegant and easily missed, this flower grows alongside germander speedwell or bird's eye, both of which, if I find them in my garden, I can scarcely bear to pull up.

The avenues and alleys between these immense trees make excellent feeding places for many small birds. They feed on insects such as craneflies, lacewings and ladybirds, as well as beech 'mast'. This is the 'fruit' of the tree, which, in days gone by, provided food for pigs; bands of the animals would be allowed to roam a forest to feed, as they still do sometimes today in the New Forest. It is

food for squirrels and jays, too, and the wood pigeon, whose voice is, to me, one of the sweetest sounds of summer rivalled only by the nightingale.

As for birch trees, they seem to spring up and form a wood anywhere, like that on Berkhamsted Common. After a fire which destroyed most of the ancient Pett's Wood at Chislehurst, Kent, silver birch grew in profusion. It used to be said that after any such woodland fire birch trees took over entirely.

In spring and summer the variety of life in a large mixed wood is enormous. You can walk through a ride and hear the banging of the spotted woodpecker ahead of you, as he drills holes into the bark of trees. You do not need to have been brought up on *The Wind in the Willows* to know that badgers live here and foxes and a variety of small animals, such as moles and wood mice. When dusk falls the tawny owl will fly from his tree-perch into the open fields to hunt for mice in the long grasses. Across the ride in the sunlight floats the speckled wood butterfly. The brimstone, the earliest butterfly to be seen, emerging in February, is like a piece of sunlight itself. Blackbirds and thrushes are singing and already sitting on eggs, while in the holes of tree trunks the coal tit will have taken up residence. In the tight woodland hedges and spinneys, linnets, hedge sparrows or dunnocks will be nesting, and the wren, no heavier than a leaf itself, will be turning over leaves for insects.

Beech avenue, remnant of Savernake Forest, Wiltshire When we try to imagine the impenetrable forest which once lay deep over so much of England, our thoughts turn to Robin Hood's Sherwood. But the forest of which Savernake was part was far older than this. The avenue was photographed in all the freshness of the awakening season. The jerky movements of nuthatches looking for insects on the bark and mossy roots of the trees caught the eye, and their boy-like whistles pierced the silent sunshine. The thin, limy soil is congenial to beeches, the principal trees of the ancient forest.

Hedges

When I lived in East Anglia in the 50s it was the custom to grub out as many hedges as possible in order to accommodate the huge pieces of modern farm machinery like the combine harvester. The destruction of hedgerows went along with that other destroyer, myxomatosis, so that the lanes were full of fallen trees and bushes, ancient blackthorn and may, as well as dead and dying rabbits. It was, for anyone but a farmer, a sad and depressing time. It seemed the end of the small, hedged field as we had always known it. Over a period of twenty years the average rate of hedgerow destruction was about 7,000 miles a year (out of an estimated total of 615,000 million miles).

Today there is a better understanding of the place the English hedge plays in the ecological history of a land; of the beauty of its formation, which includes not only the ubiquitous hawthorn, but holly, hedge maple, elder and crab apple. The hedge is now being preserved and is once more assuming its proper place in the landscape. Whereas most hedges are mechanically cut today, the

Opposite Birch trees in Epping Forest, Essex Epping, a Royal Forest, was once known as Waltham, a name meaning a forest farm settlement. Epping is famous for its hornbeams and oaks as well as silver birches.

Below A hedgerow near Ampney St Mary, Gloucestershire This hedge is conspicuous in a district of dry-stone walls. It grows on the land of an ancient manor and is probably of medieval origin.

old hawthorn hedges, legacies of the eighteenth century and the Enclosure Acts, were 'laid' every seven to ten years. The stems of the trees were half cut and woven between stakes of ash or oak. That the art is not quite forgotten can be seen in the lanes about Abercwmhir in Wales.

Before writing this section of the book I went out to examine the hedge opposite my house here in Cornwall. The road through the village encloses a grass meadow, in which sheep and lambs were running. It was 22 April and we had had a dry cold month. Indeed, it was still very cold, with frost in the early mornings. The blackthorn was out everywhere, which always means cold winds – 'blackthorn winter' they call it here, and 'plum winter' in Herefordshire.

The hedge is typically 'old' Cornish, being at least twelve feet high, of granite and slate, topped with a row of blackthorn, broken here and there by standard trees. The blackthorn is the sloe bush. If it were warmer the bees would be working the blossom. Alas, it is too cold for them and the sloe harvest (does anyone now gather them to make sloe gin?) will not be good this year.

In the length of the hedge, just twenty-five yards between two standard ash trees, I found the following: ivy; stinging nettle; jack by the hedge or garlic mustard in flower, whose leaves are excellent in salads and on which the female orange-tip butterfly lays her eggs; primroses flowering in profusion; grasses; wall pennywort; brambles – this hedge is good for blackberries later in the year; two types of fern, of which the hart's tongue is the most abundant; foxglove; germander speedwell or bird's eye in bloom; honeysuckle; cow parsley; celandine in bloom; dandelion; goosegrass; dock; red campion in bloom; stitchwort in bloom; herb robert; bracken; hedge bedstraw; bluebells; two garden escapees; a small gooseberry bush and columbines; and two fat churchyard beetles.

Opposite Beech hedge and wild **garlic**, Levens, Westmorland
This photograph celebrates the visual enchantment of a woodland floor of the starry white clusters and thick dark green leaves of the triangular-stemmed garlic.

Below left Lords and ladies
It is never possible to disregard the strange pale green hood and purple club-like centre, or to ignore the wonderful autumnal cluster of vermilion berries of this common hedgerow plant, known also as the cuckoo pint or Jack-in-the-pulpit.

Below right A hedgerow near Veryan, Cornwall
The banks of earth and stone which take the place of hedges in Cornwall, rising steeply on either side of the deep, narrow lanes, create their own specially favourable conditions of luxuriant growth and are among the great delights of the region.

Left A hedgerow to the north-west of Saffron Walden, Essex
It is a brilliant day in June after a night of showers. The strong, hollow-stemmed angelica is already succeeding the hedge-parsley, and the elder for a brief moment justifies its existence by its glorious profusion of white discs. This abundant summer landscape of the chalk, so essentially English, assumed its present form at least five centuries ago. The field path is mentioned in a survey of 1400, which also reveals that the present hedge follows the line of a large enclosure.

Above Hedgerow daisies near Kemsing, Kent
Of all the summer mixture of daisies, the ox-eye is most expressive of the season. It grows in hedges and meadows and whitens railway cuttings throughout Britain. But such a solid array as this of brilliant, glistening whiteness is not often encountered. So close are the ranks of flowers, so little grass tones them down that the bright discs seem preternaturally large. They are growing beside the road associated with Chaucer's immortal company of pilgrims.

Hedgerow, Shockerwick, Somerset
The photograph is a portrait of that vivid mid-May freshness which never fails to surprise English eyes after the long winter. The cow parsley, foaming in this Somerset hedgerow, whitens all England at this time, a spread of buttercups, such as that shining through the gap in the hedge, covers every meadow with sparkling yellow.

I have a theory about hedges such as these, close to houses and villages. It is that they are more abundant in wild flowers than those in open country. For one thing sparrows use the eaves of my house for nesting, flying to and fro from hedge to nest, depositing seeds both from my garden and from the countryside. For another cattle and sheep are frequently driven up and down the road and out through the village to pastures; sparrows and other birds, especially wrens, scavenge in the dung, and so in their turn drop the seeds of wild flowers in this fertile roadside. It might also be argued that with traffic constantly passing (and the number of dead hedgehogs we get on this road is proof of that) there is a flow of air along the hedge, which causes seeds of all kinds to fly up and be deposited amongst the grasses overgrowing the soil crevices in the granite.

Nothing lovelier than the wild rose – the common dog rose – grows in hedges.

The downy rose, its leaves covered with a soft down, is more common in the north. Wild roses often support a gall or two, which are caused by the larva of the gall wasp getting into the bud and upsetting the natural development. The result is that, instead of a flower, a kind of pin cushion is formed (country people often call it the 'robin's pin cushion'), which, although an abnormality, is attractive in itself. In some hedges the spindle, a hibernating shelter for black bean aphids, still grows. This is an old shrub of the chalk hills and has a remarkable four-lobed pink fruit in autumn.

Today one can see fine hedges of escallonia and pittosporum both in Cornwall and the Scillies, though these are mostly ornamental hedges, like those grown from tamarisk and fuchsia. Beech, too, is used in gardens and fields, though for garden hedges (where once yew was used) the most popular tree must be the *cupressus Leylandii*, which spurts away at about three feet or more a year.

Hedges, then, support a large amount of wild life and are vital to that life. They protect crops and soil from cold and winds; cattle and sheep huddle against them in the snowfalls of Wales or the north country. They were planted from necessity and by law, and have become beautiful in themselves. The oaks, elms, ash and sycamores which form the hedge standards are perhaps the most important growths in the whole landscape of Britain.

7 Rivers and Canals

Rivers

THE beginning of all rivers is a basin for rainwater, either directly from the sky or by means of land drainage and springs. Such risings are generally undistinguished in themselves, if not in their surroundings. The river Wharfe in Yorkshire, for example, begins as a small trickle in swamp ground two miles from Swarthgill, a little below Fleet Moss; the river Ure is born in springs - and usually under cloud - in the Pennines just north of the bridge at Hell Gill, and east of the Buttertubs Pass; the Thames claims two headsprings, either at Thames Head, in the parish of Coates, three miles west of Cirencester, or at Seven Springs, the headwaters of the river Churn, five miles south of Cheltenham.

Wherever a river rises the as yet small flow finds its way through the countryside, getting larger and larger until it arrives at its estuary, becomes tidal, and meets the sea. Basically, the rivers are land channels for water. Their value, where landscape is concerned, lies in what courses they take, the plant and bird life along their banks, the towns through which they pass.

A river is more interesting in its middle reaches, meandering between low hills or water-meadows, which are sometimes flooded in winter. Their banks are the home of cresses, mimulus, forget-me-not and lady's smock or cuckoo flower, so named because it flowers in mid-April, about the date the cuckoo arrives. In the shallows of rivers the frog-spawn is tangled into clumps of kingcup and yellow water-lily, the pebbles about them washed brilliantly silver or gold by the constant passing of water.

The river Stour in Suffolk is such a river; a river of water mills, the most famous being at Flatford, which is reached only when the beginning of the estuary is in sight. This is the heart of the 'Constable country'. The best time to be here is in spring. Then the river and the mill (now a naturalists' study centre) can be seen in an atmosphere much nearer to Constable's time, the elms and willows in young leaf, and not yet hanging with summer's dust.

On willows beside the Stour, as it flows through the water-meadows near Sudbury, that extraordinary butterfly, the Camberwell Beauty, has been netted. In spring and summer the air is full of the scent of meadowsweet. Where harvesting machines have not cut right up to the banks, foxgloves and ragged robin grow. The valleys of such rivers are some of the last places left in which to find wild flowers - bullrushes and yellow iris, deep plantations of comfrey,

The Thames at Twickenham, Middlesex
The Thames itself (barely tidal at this point in its course) can be glimpsed through the winter trees; the water in the foreground is overspill from the brimming river after heavy February rains. There is a special quality, which the photograph conveys, about the tranquillity and poetic melancholy of this Thames landscape. The bare deciduous trees of the London clay, the modesty and gentleness of the scene, so different from the breathtaking drama of the Wye or Severn, strike a thoroughly domestic note, but are surprising and cherished in a predominantly suburban and densely populated area. This is still the Twickenham of Pope, still the river painted by Wilson and Turner.

123

hemlock and water dropwort. And along the Cornish rivers and streams, such
as the Camel, which rides in from the sea at Padstow, there grows the spreading
Himalayan balsam. But however attractive is this orchid-like plant, it should be
kept out of gardens. I sowed seeds of it one year; the next I was swamped with
plants from the exploding seed pods.

Nevertheless, the landscape of a river (not the landscape through which it
passes, which is a different thing) is largely the wild flowers, the birds, the
heron fishing, that glorious bird the kingfisher, and in the long grasses sedge
warblers and wagtails, but above all the dragonflies. The most delicate of these
summer insects is the damosel, which loves the flowers of meadowsweet. Its
larger relative is the great green darting dragonfly, with its translucent eyes,
dodging over the surface of the water.

Here, too, is to be found that curious bird the dipper, which prefers swift-
running rivers, diving in and walking along the river bed looking for insects.
Beside the banks of calm rivers the moorhen makes its nest alongside the water
vole, whose home is actually under water. Brown trout feed here on mayfly,
eels, bream, carp, tench, stickleback – the list of both fauna and flora is almost
endless.

The most important East Anglian rivers are the Great Ouse, the Stour, the Orwell, the Deben and the Waveney, which comes to the mouth of its estuary at Lowestoft. The estuary of the river Orwell is majestic. Woods hang to the water's edge and about the mansions on the low hills opposite Pin Mill. Seen across the river, Orwell Park (now a school) and Broke Hall can reinstate for you the atmosphere of the eighteenth century. This scene of mansion, river, woods and wide skies has the elegance of the Age of Reason.

Not far from Pin Mill is Freston Tower, built of brick and rising in six stages to the angled turrets. On each floor is a single chamber; from the roof the view is magnificent, which perhaps was the reason why it was built in the mid-sixteenth century. At low tide the waters of the estuary ebb to the sea, leaving acres of mud flats, littered with dead and dying hulks long since laid up, as well as fleets of modern sailing craft.

Marsh samphire grows on these mud flats. At one time vast quantities were gathered and burned to produce soda for making soap and glass, which gave the plant its other name – glasswort. Today the countrywoman uses it for

Opposite Aysgarth Falls, Wensleydale, Yorkshire
The burst of autumn sunshine accentuates the contrast between the tremendous primeval energy of the coldly gleaming torrent and the striking irregularity of the terraces over which the Ure comes hurtling down.

Below Junction of the Greta and the Tees, Yorkshire
The bright, clear-flowing waters of the Greta and the Tees meet at this celebrated spot painted by both Cotman and Crome.

The Wharfe and the ruins of Bolton Priory, Yorkshire At this point of its course the Wharfe spreads out into the wide, calm, curving water painted by Turner. Because monasteries were of necessity sited close to water, abbey ruins often play an important part in the composition of a river landscape. Tintern, Fountains and Shap come immediately to mind, joined in our recollection with their picturesquely reflected counterparts. At Bolton the pastoral setting of the ruins by the sweep of the river movingly contrasts with the severity of the distant moors.

making pickle. Some of the finest samphire came from the flats opposite the Cliff Quay Power Station, which in certain lights, here beside the river, could be mistaken for a palace on the outskirts of Ipswich. The river Orwell at this point passes through the town. Further inland, and nearer its source, it becomes the Gipping, on whose banks the poet John Milton must have walked when he was staying with his tutor, Dr Young, at Stowmarket. Today he would hardly recognize the place because of the A45, which runs from Felixstowe to Birmingham.

'There is a frontier line to civilization in this country yet', wrote Richard Jefferies, the naturalist, 'and not far outside its great centres we come quickly, even now, on the borderland of nature. Modern progress, except where it has exterminated them, has scarcely touched the habits of birds and animals; so up to the very metropolis the nightingale yearly returns to her former haunts.'

That was written in 1870, describing the outskirts of London. No longer is it true of London, despite all the 'modern' improvements in pesticides, pollution, traffic and massive roads. But it is still true of the upper reaches of rivers like the Stour especially about Sudbury and Haverhill where it runs through thickets. It is true also of those Norfolk rivers, such as the Wissey or the Nar, where the

Peddars Way comes down from Hunstanton to Castle Acre, or the river Bure through the Broads, or the little river Dove through the town of Eye.

The Dove is not a great river. Perhaps it is no more than a stream flowing into the Waveney, but it is the epitome of all small streams that go to swell the Suffolk rivers. Quite natural, therefore, to hear the nightingale near it. And by roadsides, such as those linking the reservoir at Abberton and the town of Colchester, I have stood under the hedges, with traffic whizzing by, and watched the nightingale singing at noon. I could have reached out and touched that brown bird, for this is nightingale country, and even with the expansion of Colchester and the traffic to Mersea Island, nothing puts off its return from year to year.

Of all Yorkshire rivers I love best perhaps the Ure, because of the dramatic ruins which stand beside it. Not that the river itself is undramatic. At Aysgarth Falls, when I last saw it the river was in full spate, peat-coloured, the water coming down swiftly between green fields and high woods, crashing over the rocks in wild cascades, grey wagtails darting over its banks after insects.

I had come from Muker over Buttertubs Pass through rain and low cloud to the river. This treeless pass joins the river Swale to the Ure, with Great Shunner

The Eden at Appleby, Westmorland
The tumbled rocks of the Eden's course between magnificent escarpments above Appleby have vanished from this placid stretch of the river. Its name, 'fetch'd from Paradise', as Wordsworth said, comes from the Celtic root *don*, meaning water or river, and is a significant survival in a region where Anglian and Norse settlements largely obliterated the Celts. The autumn mist lingering on the richly wooded hill beyond the simple bridge (which looks 18th century but was actually built in 1889) with its single figure deepens the exquisite repose of the scene.

The Estuary of the Dwyryd, Merioneth
It joins the estuary of the Glaslyn where the low tide leaves vast stretches of sand, some of it quaking, some of it firm and golden, laced by shallow rivulets and deep, treacherous streams, one of them swirling about a tiny island. It is possible, with cunning, to walk across the double estuary or to reach the open sea, where the line of foam seems to be above one's head. Very soon the grand Miltonian landscape of mountains, trees and rocky coves and sandy shelves recedes into the distance, an insignificant backcloth to the drama of wind and water. There are few shells on the exposed, endless flats, but many bleached, incredibly fragile skeletons of seabirds and the delicate, star-patterned, bubble-light remains of sea urchins. Sandpipers and screaming gulls accompany the walker, and every now and then he encounters parties of striking, pink-legged, black and white shelduck.

Fell, 2,340 feet, on the left, and Lovely Seat, 2,213 feet, on the right. The twisting road is spaced with tall poles every twenty yards or so, guides above snow-drifts, and obviously very necessary in winter. The 'buttertubs' themselves are a number of deep limestone shafts lying near the roadside and dangerous, too, in winter.

At Hawes you cross the Ure, and from the Aysgarth Falls you come through Wensleydale, with Castle Bolton on your left. Here Mary Queen of Scots was incarcerated for some time. The dungeons and armourer's smithy alone would qualify this to be called 'a grim pile'. Set back from the road and river on its hill, this fortress is mirrored in that natural fortress opposite, Penhill Beacon.

The river passes by the ruined Middleham Castle, the favourite home of Richard III, and a stronghold even today. And on past beautiful Jervaulx Abbey, set in a pastoral landscape, as are all the ruined abbeys in Yorkshire. Jervaulx, like Fountains, is surrounded by trees, the sun lighting up the broken masonry, the ruins abundant with wild flowers. Perhaps the most wonderful part is the ruined Chapter House. Seen at the time when the light is beginning to lose the false brilliance that comes after sundown, these ruins take on a new life, and become a romantic scene haunted by ghosts from the past.

Not far away is the town of Masham, with its cross in the centre of a vast cobbled market-place, where once some forty thousand sheep were brought for sale in front of the King's Head Hotel, itself an old posting house. Masham is a permanent feature of the landscape, with its rounded stone archways, wide enough to take a coach, leading to stables between the buildings. Here the Ure, having come through Wensleydale, runs beneath a four-arched bridge, built in 1754, and on to Ripon and Boroughbridge, where it joins the river Ouse. The banks beside the playing-fields are lined with deep-red Himalayan balsam beneath tall trees.

To see a great river in all its beauty one would hardly go to the north-east of England, for the Tyne, the Wear and the Tees, to say nothing of the Mersey on the west coast, are more celebrated for population explosion, industry and pollution. For this beauty one has to go to the upper reaches of the river Aire, or to the river Derwent in Borrowdale, swirling over the rapids, its banks clustered with trees. To view the most dramatic rivers you must go even further north, into Scotland, to the salmon rivers, to the red deer seen in winter on the banks of the river Dee, where it twists and turns below the forests of Braemar, or to the river Garry, running down the Pass of Killiecrankie, beneath the railway viaduct and the pointed peak of Ben-y-Gloe.

The river Clyde, which starts from a spring in the Lowther Hills, and then runs via the Daer Dam (reservoir for Lanarkshire) to Water Meetings, falls into the categories of both pastoral and industrial landscape. Indeed the landscape of the upper Clyde might be in southern England, running through soft hills, orchards and farmsteads, before reaching the hydro-electric works at the Falls of Clyde. In a short distance the whole river scene changes. It becomes in-dustrialized at Motherwell and Wishaw and the fourteen miles of the Glasgow

The photograph well records
the character of this pastoral
river as it appears through
the greater part of its noble
course: it flows, clear and
full, between smooth,
swelling hills and through
luxuriant meadows and
groves. This gentle valley
was peculiarly vulnerable to
attack by marauding English-
men and the feudal
proprietors built defensive
castles along the river
banks. Neidpath was the
residence of the powerful
Border family of Fraser.

Opposite Hornbeam and
beech in winter, near Saffron
Walden, Essex

docks. And so to Clydebank and John Brown's shipyard, where some of the
world's greatest ships have been launched.

The finest stretches of river, from the point of view of pure water and landscape, are to be seen in the interior of the country, in Scotland, in the Lake
District, in Yorkshire, in Wales and the West Country.

A river may be many things, from a highway into the surrounding countryside to a paradise for fishermen, but its most important function, in landscape
at least, is refreshment. This is particularly true of such rivers as the Glaslyn,
running in its rapids and falls through woods by the town of Beddgelert in
Caernarvonshire. Falls and rapids are a feature of these mountain streams
lighting the whole landscape. Where the Afon Wen joins the Mawddach the
water is sparkling and alive beneath the green Douglas firs and rugged oaks of
the forests of Coed-y-brenin.

In Lyn Conway, high on Migneint, one of the loveliest and most dramatic
rivers, the Conway, begins its journey to the sea. Past the Swallow Falls at
Betws-y-coed, the river opens out into the wide valley beside the castle at
Llanrwst with mountains in the distance, and so to its estuary and to the castle
at Conway itself.

Even higher than the source of the river Conway, at Y Dault (the Black Height), another river Dee rises in Merionethshire and flows through Bala Lake, through the green vales of Edeyrnion and Llangollen eventually to reach Chester. And still in Wales, it is possible to walk through the spruce woods of Hafren Forest and the gorse below the Pen y Carreg rocks, along forest roads to a peat-bog on the slopes of Plynlimon, some 2,000 feet above sea-level.

Standing here with little but the sheep feeding and a buzzard flying overhead, it is incredible to think that this trickle of water will become a great river when, at last, it flows beneath that magnificent new Severn Bridge, near the village of Aust, or opening out into the Bristol Channel and the holiday 'delights' of Weston-super-Mare. The Severn, the Teme and the Wye all rise in the mountains of mid-Wales within a few miles of each other. But what different rivers they are! The Severn is 'dark and powerful', a river of towns and cities; the Teme, a rural river of orchards and hop-yards; and the Wye, the queen of large rivers, is everything the others are and much more.

The Wye runs into the great reservoirs of the Elan Valley through the tall hills, past Newbridge on Wye, and so to Builth Wells, clear and clean beneath the trees, where once the railway line ran beside it, until it comes to Hay-on-Wye and the Golden Valley. The landscape of this part of the river is made up of woodlands and small deserted lanes. To the north-east, on the river Ithon, a tributary of the Wye, is that Edwardian town, Llandrindod Wells, where one can drink the waters and expect to meet the ghost of Edward VII round every corner.

Opposite Urquhat Castle, Loch Ness, Inverness-shire

Left The Teifi near Pontrhydfendigaid, Cardiganshire
The river rises in a lake amid the bogs of Tregaron. Pontrhydfendigaid is but one of a number of small market towns strung along its course, but the river is most memorable for scenes such as this, where, a stream of shallows and deep pools, it waters a remote pastoral landscape of continually changing light. Salmon and the migratory trout known as the sewin are fished in the Teifi and it is said that the last haunt of the beaver is along its banks. On the lower reaches of the river men still fish in coracles, little wicker boats which have not changed since the Romans curiously observed and described them.

The Severn from Nympsfield,
Gloucestershire
This view of the Vale of
Gloucester and the Severn
estuary in stormy, luminous
mood imparts an urgent
sense of the mystery and
antiquity of the landscape,
still deeply rural, speckled
with forest remnants and in
spring yellow with wild
daffodils. A long-barrow
tomb lies close to the point
on the escarpment from
which the photograph was
taken, commanding the
outlook towards the
formidable river with its
rushing tides and dangerous
currents. From here it is
possible to watch the
immense rise in the height of
the water, some 18 ft, and
occasionally nearly three
times as much, which
accompanies the famous
tidal bore of the Severn.
When the high spring tide
meets the flow of the river,
the rapidly gaining bulk of
the seawater creates a great
wave which roars and rushes
upstream. It is not surprising
that the Celtic god of the
estuary, Noadu, survived
the Roman occupation to be
worshipped under the name
Nodens and to be repre-
sented on Romano-British
ornaments as mounted on a
car drawn by seahorses
riding majestically on the
crest of the Severn bore.

So the Wye comes down, in all its silvan beauty, past Goodrich Castle, where Wordsworth met the little girl who inspired his poem 'We are Seven', and into its narrow gorge at the beauty spot of Symond's Yat. The river here flows into that mighty loop which runs for five miles beneath the woods to encircle Huntsman Hill and then flows back to within a few hundred yards of its first course. In the hills above the river is King Arthur's Cave, where the relics of men and women who lived twenty thousand years ago were discovered. The river then runs through Monmouth and past the most beautiful of all Cistercian ruins, Tintern Abbey, amongst wooded hills, with the sun pouring through the tall ruined arches of the nave and, at last, to its joining with the river Severn under the new road bridge.

Once across this majestic bridge you are in the West Country, looking towards that other modern bridge over the river Tamar, which divides Devon and Cornwall, or towards the river Tavy, flowing down from its source on Black Ridge on Dartmoor, through the old stannary town of Tavistock till it joins the Tamar just above Saltash and the bridge.

It hardly matters which of these lovely West Country rivers you choose, the landscape is rarely anything but perfect. They run mostly from the heights of the moors – Dartmoor, Exmoor or Bodmin Moor – like the river Fowey, which

Above The Wye at Lancaut, Monmouthshire
This view of the Wye shows the exciting conformation of this most glorious of meandering rivers and reveals the way in which such a river sculpts the land. As it swings from side to side it causes erosion on the concave side and deposits sandbanks on the convex side.

Opposite The Tamar from Morwell Rocks, Cornwall
The Celtic name of the river dividing Cornwall from Devon means 'quiet and spreading river'. An extraordinary feature of the Tamar is that it runs inland from the sea, for it rises near the Bristol Channel and flows south.

The Tavy near Tamerton
Foliot, Devon
The Tavy is here approaching its mouth which, beyond
the railway bridge, it shares
with the Tamar. The source
of the river is on Dartmoor;
it flows through a deep valley
to Tavistock and before
it enters these calm tidal
reaches its course is broken
by huge rocks, waterfalls
and eddying bays. The single
pylon on the estuary of the
two rivers adds a vertical
accent of the 20th century to
the landscape.

has its beginning under Brown Willy, the highest tor in Cornwall, while the
river Camel runs from the west side of Bodmin Moor, through the woods and
falls of Dunmere Forest until it joins the sea at the Doom Bar at Padstow. The
streams about St Austell run white with the effluent of the china clay mines and
come down into the harbour of Charlestown in St Austell Bay. And by the
beautiful wooded Helford river, north of Goonhilly Downs, the landscape is
now dominated by the dishes of Telstar, high above the heather and gorse and
the chittering stonechats that nest here.

The characteristic of these rivers is intimacy, from the shallow wooded falls
at Golytha on the Fowey, to the tumbling rivers of Dartmoor crossed by
ancient clapper bridges. In a landscape of rock and tor the rivers are filled with
boulders and brown water from the moorland peat, like the West Dart at
Hexworthy, or the little streams of the Barle and the Exe which rise in Exmoor
National Park. They flow over the moor between hills purple with heather and
green with woodlands.

I never took much notice of the river Thames in its lower reaches, although I
was born just outside London. It was too big, too full of traffic and too dirty.
But like all boys, then and today, I had a favourite stream, the river Darent.
Admittedly, this ran into the Thames, but to me it means Kent and rivers
because it first introduced me to river life beneath the trees of its valley at
Eynsford, where the artist Samuel Palmer painted many of his landscapes.

I have lived in the West Country for years and admire and honour its rivers,
but it is the memories of childhood that make me go back to those Sussex rivers,
the Adur and the Arun. For this is, perhaps, the best quality of streams as
opposed to rivers – they form the study of landscape for the young, whether it
be for their flora and fauna, for their fishing, or their boating. For all ages
rivers are the moving wonder of landscape.

Canals

For anyone who does not know the canals their narrowness comes as a surprise.
Unlike rivers, canal waters hardly move at all, and the maximum flow, if it is
to remain under control, must not exceed half a mile an hour.

Travelling from the West Country to London, I can see from the train one of
the loveliest of all British canals, the Kennet and Avon. With its small locks it
looks, in sunlight, no more than a silver drain as it goes from Bristol to Bath and
so, via Devizes, to Newbury and Reading, where it joins the Thames.

By virtue of the fact that they were built to run, where possible, along the
contours of the land, the canals pass through exquisite pastoral scenery. In
places they may rise very high, like the Leeds and Liverpool Canal where it
winds round the top of the Pennines, near East Marton. Later, under the influence of Telford, canals were cut to go straight across the country. By then
engineers had developed methods for lock-building, aqueducts, and tunnels.

Even when it is necessary for a canal to cross a valley by means of an aqueduct, such as that where the Llangollen Canal crosses the Dee valley at Pont Cysyllte, three and a half miles east of Llangollen, the landscape is of woods and water. On this confined waterway, one of Telford's greatest engineering feats, completed in 1805, you are so high as to be in the tops of the trees themselves.

Canals, of course, were built for industrial reasons. It is inevitable, then, that the largest network lies in the Midlands. The Birmingham canals are reached from London by a waterway now known under the blanket name of the Grand Union, part of which is the old Grand Junction, which ran from Brentford to Braunston, in the Midlands. Before it was completed, independent canals were built linking it in a direct line to Warwick and Birmingham. Later the Regent's Canal connected the Middlesex end to Limehouse and the London docks.

Although the water moves slowly, canals must still be fed in order to keep the water-level constant. The Tring Reservoirs were built to supply the Grand Junction Canal, and these waters are now famous for black tern, crested grebe and other wild-fowl. The Birmingham Canal is fed by the Edgbaston reservoir, created from Roach Pool at Rotton Park. At one end there are willow trees; at the other you look out over Spring Hill to an industrial landscape.

So, from dockland London, this canal threads its way along the pleasant Northamptonshire countryside, joining the river Nene at Northampton itself. At Foxton in Leicestershire there are two famous staircases of five locks each; while at Torksey the Fosdyke Navigation runs south-east from the Trent to Lincoln, where it continues as the Witham Navigation to Boston. The Fosdyke dates from the Roman occupation; it is the oldest artificially constructed waterway in Britain.

Canal-building is responsible for many impressive engineering feats, such as the Acton Swing Bridge over the Weaver Navigation, set in a landscape of lawns and neat houses, joining the roads across the canal; or the Western Point Docks on the same navigation; or the enormous Anderton Boat Lift which raises and lowers boats fifty feet and joins the river Weaver, near Northwich, to the high-level Trent and Mersey Canal.

To understand the vastness of these engineering feats, stand and watch a tanker entering the Gloucester and Sharpness Canal; or coal barges from the Yorkshire pits going down to a power station on the Aire and Calder Navigation. Look down at Bingley Five Rise on the Leeds and Liverpool Canal, which lifts boats fifty-nine feet up its lock-staircase, and you have before you a fine landscape of country running into an industrial area by means of this channel of water. The deep green of the heavy-leaved trees shades off into the tall towers of factories and warehouses.

In the end one returns to the tow paths and what can be seen on them. Something like three million anglers fish from these paths, and nearly a million more people use them for walking, painting, and studying the flora and fauna. One returns to places like East Marton on the Leeds and Liverpool Canal, where the tow path forms part of the Pennine Way footpath; or to the Royal Military

Towards Lincoln from Tattershall Bridge, Lincolnshire
The subject of this late summer moonlit scene is as much sky as river. Power lines and wires are absorbed as effortlessly as trees and hedges into the silent splendid cloudscape and its brilliant reflection in the slow-moving Witham. It is the Lincolnshire of 'the waste, enormous marsh', of great distances and wide expanses which Tennyson so often described:
'Where from the frequent bridge
Like emblems of infinity
The trenched waters runs from sky to sky.'
This landscape was well drained and extensively settled in Romano-British times. Not far from this point Roman engineers constructed the canal known as Fosdyke to connect the Witham with the Trent at Torksey.

The Trent at Kelham,
Nottinghamshire
The picturesque traveller
Gilpin ignored Nottinghamshire, and it is not a county
which springs immediately
to mind in a consideration
of the countryside of Britain.
Yet it inspired D. H. Lawrence to write some of the
most poignant and vivid
descriptions of the English
landscape in our literature.
This quiet view of the Trent,
taken in the haze of early
morning at midsummer,
contains all the elements,
the browsing cattle and lush
meadows, the tranquil
reflections, even the typical
Lombardy poplars which we
associate with English rivers.
Near the scene of the
photograph, as English, but
affording the sharpest
contrast to the serene river
landscape in its aggressive,
repellent shape and material,
is George Gilbert Scott's
Kelham Hall. Geologically
the Trent is interesting
because it once flowed east
from Nottingham but was
constrained by the ice
barrier of the Third
Glaciation to curve north
to Newark after forming a
huge lake known as Lake
Humber.

Canal in Kent, built in Napoleonic times as a coastal defence. At Hythe the canal is bordered by gardens to form a double artificial landscape, and runs all the way to the sea at Rye, fringed by trees. This canal actually converts Romney Marsh into an island.

For me there is no more exciting 'landscape' project than the restoration of canals. Not only does it provide extra possibilities for leisure use, in boating, walking, and even in the actual work of restoration by voluntary co-operation, but it gives enormous scope for improving the landscape itself by tree-planting and the preservation of canal 'curiosities'.

There is a fine example of such a 'curiosity' at Drayton Bassett, where the old canal footbridge is poised between two castellated towers. They look slightly grotesque beyond the entrance to Manor Park. They were, no doubt, built in this way to set off the actual park gates and lodge. Another 'curiosity' of canal construction is preserved at King's Norton, where the guillotine lock once controlled the water supply on the Worcester and Birmingham Canal and the Stratford-upon-Avon Canal. Beyond its bridge it looks very much like some colossal machine used in the French Revolution to cut off the heads of aristocrats. Although no longer used, the winches are still in good condition.

At Wordsley the Stuart Crystal bottle kiln still stands beside the Stourbridge Canal like an early cooling tower. It is now preserved as an industrial monument. A new lease of life has been given to the boats on the Birmingham canals at Bilston in the Black Country. They are used for a very modern purpose – the carrying of pipes needed to supply natural gas to the West Midlands, which are being laid under the tow path.

One of the most interesting canal-restoration schemes is that of the Grand Western Canal, built between 1811 and 1814, and closed to traffic in 1924. In May 1971 the Devon County Council took over from British Waterways responsibility for the eleven miles between Tiverton and Holcombe Rogus, with the idea of turning it into a country park.

If you start at the canal basin at Tiverton, you can see the remains of the lime kilns. In the days before modern artificial fertilizers the canal was mainly used for carrying limestone from Canonsleigh quarries at Holcombe Rogus. This was burnt with coal to produce agricultural lime, so extensively used in the first half of the nineteenth century.

A walk along the tow path takes you through delightful landscape scenery as the canal winds above the valley of the river Loman, lined with tall oak trees. At Manley Bridge one can still see the old stonemason's marks. Shortly after the bridge is an aqueduct consisting of a cast-iron trough supported on two cast-iron arches, enclosed in brickwork. At Halberton, in this tree-scattered plain to the south, the canal crosses the Change Path Bridge, from which one can see the willows and sycamores overhanging that curious pond at Halberton, which is reputed never to have frozen over.

The next bridge, Greenway, is constructed of dressed sandstone, proof of the former use of the quarries a mile ahead. The canal wanders down to Sampford Peverell and the brick bridge, the courses being set at an angle to the

base, this being a skew-bridge, crossing the canal diagonally. Half a mile from the canal, below Ayshford, there is an interesting mill. The axle of the water-wheel can be seen housed beneath a projection from the mill itself, and the runaway sluice mechanism is still intact.

And so to Fernacre where, on the side opposite the tow path, a spring comes into the canal and provides one of its water sources. At Whipcott, just beyond the bridge, there are more lime kilns and two cottages where horses once were shod. A path opposite leads to an overgrown wharf. The restored part of the canal ends at Loudwells beside Lock's Cottage.

Restorations such as this can be found all over the countryside, on what are known as the 'Remainder' Waterways, under the care of the British Waterways Board. The odd thing about such work is that it costs less to restore a canal than to fill it in.

The canals, then, are sedate highways about the country, the banks of which are much favoured by wild life, especially when they run through cuttings where hawthorns and other bushes are not regularly cut. In this respect they are much like cuttings on deserted railway lines which have been left wild and overgrown. Such places, in the same way as deserted quarries, are a paradise for the naturalist.

Boat traffic on a canal does not seem to disturb the bullfinches, greenfinches, chaffinches, pipits, yellow hammers, nightingales and warblers which nest and feed here. Where sedges grow tall enough to reach the overhanging branches of hawthorn, sedge warblers sing night and day. You can often find the nests of reed buntings in low bushes at the water's edge. The cock bird looks very fine in his breeding colours with his white collar and jet-black head. At dusk, when the canal water is calmer and more sedate, a hedgehog will come to the bank to drink and to hunt for its food of snails, slugs and worms.

The Grand Junction Canal at Grove, Buckinghamshire
The English landscape was almost as much affected by the creation of canals, between 1760 and 1825, as by the later introduction of the railways. Innumerable hump bridges, many of them, like the one in this photograph, of great charm, cuttings, embankments, aqueducts, tunnels and locks and winding or unnaturally straight ribbons of water, dark and polluted in industrial areas, clear and sparkling in the open country, transformed the scene and brought changes in bird and plant life as well as in man's environment. The humble subject of the photograph, with its glimpse of sluice and lock and the former lock-keeper's house, is more truly evocative of canal landscape than spectacular structures such as Telford's bridge over the deeply cut Shropshire Union Canal or Rennie's great aqueduct over the Lune.

8 Sea-shore and Coastline

THE landscape of the sea-shore is made up of rocks, sands or pebbles with, here and there, a large inlet for a river. The colour of this landscape is in the rock and sand, in the green of grass headlands, and in the variety of shells littering the shore. The birds which haunt and nest in the crannies of unclimbable cliff faces divide the whole picture by their moving flight-paths, above the delicacy of wild flowers and seaweeds.

Above all these wonders stand lighthouses and castles, in use or in ruins, neolithic camps, weather-beaten farmhouses, and in Cornwall, the ruined engine-houses of disused tin mines. In the main the sea-coast is a rugged landscape except where, in places such as Camber Sands in Sussex, the land is at the same level, or lower than the sea. Long stretches of sand, as at Pendine in Wales, pebble beaches like Chesil Beach in Dorset, or at Brighton in Sussex or on the east coast at Bawdsey, are variations in the total landscape of the 6,000-mile coastline.

No doubt if you are a sailing man and own a boat, the best way of seeing the coast is to sail round it. But to do so would give you no more than a glimpse of the nature of the shore, except when you put into a harbour. The best way of all is to walk along selected areas of shore such as the Island of Hoy in the Orkneys, where the Old Man of Hoy, an immense pointed rock, rises 450 feet above the sea. This spectacular walk, along the cliffs west and north of Rackwick and its long sandy bay, is one of the most dramatic in Britain. Here on the cliffs razorbills, puffins and guillemots breed. A landscape remote from the calmer, more peaceful ones of the south, it is more akin to Wales and the West Country.

It is different, too, from the sand dunes and sandy beaches of Northumbria, especially that beach of white sand below the red sandstone of Bamburgh Castle. The walls of this castle, and the rocks upon which it is built, form an impregnable fortress 150 feet high, with the sea swirling in at its feet.

Opposite are the Farne Islands, a major bird sanctuary and the breeding-ground of grey seals. The National Trust now cares for the twenty-five islands in the group. On the furthest island, Longstone, with its famous lighthouse, Grace Darling lived and rowed out to perform her celebrated rescue in 1838. Here, too, is the shallow estuary of Budle Bay, which is only covered by water at high tide. These marshes, the haunt of wild-fowl, duck, pink-footed geese and oyster catchers, are looked after by the Lindisfarne National Nature

Bamburgh, Northumberland
The dark, pungent piles of grass-wrack and tangleweed flung up on the white sandy beach make a splendid foil to the red sandstone castle standing on an eminence which is ideal for a fortification. It is an outcrop of the famous Whinsill, the great intrusion of volcanic rock which stretches from Burton Fell on the Pennine escarpment to beyond the Farne Islands. The castle heightens the drama of the solitary dune-girt shore. Its picturesque outline is due to imaginative rebuilding in the 18th century and further restoration at the end of Victoria's reign. When the Bishop of Durham acquired the Norman castle in 1704, ruin had claimed every part of it. The Bishop's trustee Dr Sharp rebuilt the keep for use as a school, an infirmary, a granary and lodgings for shipwrecked sailors, and set a lighthouse on top of it.

Opposite The Cliffs, Hunstanton, Norfolk

Below Holkham Beach, Norfolk
The photograph was taken towards sunset when the distant pinewoods showed like a dark stain beyond the vast and luminous expanse of sand. The tide recedes for two miles leaving continually changing flats of curved, ridged and rippled sand reflecting the sky, the white breasts of gulls and the darting flight of the sandpiper.

Reserve. And just south, in Yorkshire, is the Cleveland Way footpath, which skirts the National Park for 120 miles, for most of its length along the foreshore.

If, in fact, you were walking the entire coastline, you would come to the nature trail at Gibraltar Point on The Wash, where curlews, terns, skuas and snow buntings can be observed. The Wash itself is a huge area of 300 square miles of shallow sea. Though I have only seen The Wash in calm weather, when its sands, at low tide, stretch for miles, they say that the north-east wind can turn this inland sea into a raging ocean. The fenland church of Boston (The Stump) can be seen from all angles, standing high above the marshes and sand flats of The Wash, and the highly cultivated land at its edges.

This is a landscape of fen and broad, in which old Caister Castle stands out. The castle was built *c.* 1432 by Sir John Fastolf, who led the English archers at Agincourt. Built in the form of a quadrangle, the most impressive remains are the high circular tower and the walls rising sheer from the wide moat. Windows

still look out on its dark moat water; the black shapes of rook and jackdaw are now the only sentinels, and flowers, especially pellitory of the wall and ivy-leaved toadflax, are to be found growing in the brickwork.

All along this coast are such haunted places. At Dunwich, below Walberswick and the Westward marshes, was once a populous city with 'fifty-two churches', all now under the sea. The glory that is gone hangs over these crumbling cliffs and about Dunwich Wood itself, just back from the shoreline, which was once the garden of the monastery. Sometimes on the sand and pebble beach you can still pick up bones washed from the graveyard of the last church to tumble from the cliff top into the sea. It is a sad and lonely place, adorned, here and there, with that delicate wild flower, the Dunwich rose.

All along this shingle coast, each side of Woodbridge Haven, where the Deben meets the sea, and at Bawdsey, where the beach is of dark-red shingle, there are martello towers. They were built to defend the coastline against Napoleon's threatened invasion, and were used to house French prisoners of war. The solid masonry supported a gun battery on a platform at the top, with two or three guns to fire over a low parapet. Many of these empty towers now

Opposite Bluebells in the New Forest, Hampshire

Below Martello Tower between Shingle Street and Bawdsey, Suffolk
Like the forts of the Saxon Shore the Martello towers were built as a defence against invasion. They were constructed 1810–12 by the Royal Engineers and were named after the Torre della Martella in Corsica which had played a part in the campaign of 1784. This close-up view gives a sense of the excitement aroused by the huge round chess-castle shapes in this lonely, low-lying, sea-wracked terrain.

The beach, Hastings,
Sussex
The fishing boats and carts
on the shingle beach are
familiar images in Victorian
seaside photographs. They
recall the history of Hastings
before it was developed as a
popular resort. It was
originally the most important
of the Cinque ports and
until the late Middle Ages,
when trade began to decline,
supplied and manned ships
in both peace and war and
was engaged in herring
fishing off the Norfolk coast.
At the time of its revival as a
seaside town, Hastings had
sadly decayed, though it was
still and has remained a
fishing port.

provide nesting-places for swallows. At Sizewell, standing on the edge of the beach like some fortress of another kind, is the nuclear power station.

Many things have been 'beachcombed' at Bawdsey, from barrels of wine to amber found among clusters of horned poppy growing about the decayed pillboxes of the Second World War. In winter these beaches are lonely, the east wind banging against wooden breakwaters, the sea curling its waves in vast cylinders of water, sucking away old pebble ridges, creating new. This is the prevailing sound of such beaches, the drift of pebbles up and down, beneath the cries of herring gulls and the never-ending fall of the sea.

To the south the red crag cliffs of Walton on the Naze are full of fossils, and beneath the sea are the ruins of a castle, while on Walton Backwaters, reached only from the sea, geese, purple sandpipers and skuas congregate. The coast-line here is interrupted by the estuaries of the rivers Colne, the Blackwater and the Crouch. At Bradwell-on-Sea are the twin grey towers of yet another nuclear power station, which are becoming as numerous as castles round the coast. And so to Maplin Sands, close to the holiday resort of Southend-on-Sea and the rivers Thames, Medway and Swale. At Swalecliffe I have dug the teeth of mammoth and other fossils from the shore mud, and walked via Herne Bay to Reculver, where the twin towers of the ruined church which King Egbert of

Kent raised in AD 669 inside a third-century Roman fort, stand on the sea's edge like mariners' guides.

There is no end to these seaboard fortifications, from the three Tudor castles at Sandown, Deal and Walmer, to that at Dover, above the famous white cliffs, looking down on the treacherous Goodwin Sands, to Camber castle, which was actually on the coast when Henry VIII built it, but now that the sea has retreated is a mile inland.

Beachy Head is 532 feet up from the sea; to the west are the Seven Sisters, seven rounded chalk cliffs belonging to the National Trust. We are, once again, in a landscape of holiday towns below the South Downs – Brighton, Worthing and Middleton or Littlehampton, where a swing bridge carries the A259 over the swift-running river Arun. It is a landscape, too, of holiday harbours with their thousands of colourful sails, and sailing rivers such as the Hamble, off Southampton Water. From the wooded shores of the Beaulieu river you come to the broad, gentle sands of Weymouth, where in 1789 George III was the first King of England to use a bathing-machine.

At Chesil Beach, eighteen miles of graded pebbles on the Dorset coast, is Abbotsbury, one of the country's most famous bird sanctuaries. Enclosed on

Brighton, Sussex, in winter
At this time of year the cosmopolitan pleasure resort is dramatically transformed. Storms blow up from the south-west and the sea shows its primitive power, drenching the stucco façades with spray, crashing its millions of tons of weight upon pier and pebbles. Once a fishing village called Brightelmstone, Brighton became a holiday town long before it was patronized by the Prince of Wales, later George IV. As early as the 18th century Dr Richard Russell discovered a chalybeate spring in St Anne's well and started the whole idea of the seaside resort.

The beach at Newhaven,
Sussex
The child stands on the edge
of a sea like pale-green silk
fringed with the narrowest
lace of foam; the slow sails
of the dinghies melt into the
pearly distances of the
halcyon July afternoon. This
is the seaside of one's childhood, a place of tangy, salty
air, a place associated with
the sweet transitory pleasures
of paddling, shell-hunting,
donkey rides, sand pies and
moated fortresses.

the salt-water lake, the swannery is best seen in the spring when the birds are
nesting. A little further west is the romantic scenery of the Landslip. These
steep clay cliffs are generally unstable, and small falls occur every year. The last
of the great landslips occurred in 1839, when eight million tons of soil fell into
the sea leaving a massive cleft now filled with woodlands and vegetation. One
can walk in the 400-foot-wide ravine for half a mile and hardly realize that the
sea is so near. Badgers live here in this Undercliff National Nature Reserve;
nightingales sing and nest above lizards basking in the sun. It is recorded that
400 species of wild flower have been found here.

Once again the landscape opens to rivers – the Exe, the Teign and the Dart.
As the train from Paddington to Penzance passes Dawlish Warren and the town,
the tall red cliffs and tunnels enclose it on one side, the sea on the other. It
makes a most satisfactory and romantic introduction to the coasts of the West
Country, to the pink sands of Paignton, or the steep, shelving beach of white

pebbles at Exbury Cove, to Goodshelter, with its cove surrounded by trees, or Prawle Point, where ships of all kinds can be seen from the headland, from ocean-going liners to tankers and container ships.

And so we come to Plymouth, the Sound, and the river Tamar dividing Devon from Cornwall, where the coast path runs from Mount Edgcumbe Country Park in the south, westwards to round the Land's End, and finishes in the north-east, beyond Bude, at Marshland Mouth. This is one of the longest and most dramatic of seascape walks in Britain, and it would be impossible here to note every beauty spot on the way. It takes in both the gentle beauty of the Fowey estuary, and the Helford river, with their southern climate and woods and sub-tropical vegetation found, too, in the Scillies. It passes the lovely town of Falmouth and those enchanting coves about the Lizard – Coverack, Church Cove, Kynance and Mullion – where in spring the headland grass is covered with wild flowers, blue squills, sea pink or thrift, bloody cranesbill, and mesembryanthemum. The headlands themselves are the nesting-

The Chesil Bank, Dorset
Apart from the fine spread at Orford Ness and Shingle Street in Suffolk, this extraordinarily high, unbroken ridge of shingle, stretching 18 miles from Bridport to the Isle of Portland, is the most extensive accumulation of shingle in the world.

Gradually built up by ocean currents, it probably grew from a bar to a lengthening ridge, eventually joining the Isle of Portland to the mainland and enclosing between itself and the shore the shallow lagoon known as the Fleet.

places of gulls, cormorants and shags. This is the warm south-west coast dominated by Penzance and St Michael's Mount, connected to the town by a causeway at low tide.

When the path turns about on itself at Land's End, it takes on the hardness, the awesomeness, of high granite rocks at Zennor Cliffs, running up past the lonely sand flats of Hayle to the sheer cliffs of St Agnes, and the long rollers of the sandy beach at Perranporth. Beyond the summer playground of Newquay the solitary stones of Bedruthan Steps stand in acres of sand at low tide. The only sound is the echo of the foghorn from Trevose Head and the sea running over the Doom Bar at Padstow, the grave of many a ship in the past, from brigantines to coasting schooners. This dangerous sandbar is never still. When westerly gales sweep into the estuary of the river Camel, on which Padstow stands, past Stepper Point and Trevose Head, no one but the most experienced local fisherman can be absolutely sure where the Doom Bar will be, or in what quantity.

The coast path goes on into the tiny fishing village of Port Isaac, and to the beauty of Trebarwith Strand with its fearsome rocks decorated at low tide

Opposite Kimmeridge Bay, Dorset
The bay gave its name to the thick Kimmeridge clays which were formed when the greater part of Britain was submerged beneath the muddy Jurassic sea.

Below Tresco, Isles of Scilly
In Scillonia there is no certain boundary between wild and cultivated flowers. Of the foreign plants introduced into the Tresco Abbey gardens many have established themselves as natives. The commonest of such plants is that shown in the photograph – the mesembryanthemum.

Near Scalloway, Mainland,
Shetland Isles
There are no long shadows
athwart the rough beach
and bright water although it
is evening. The light has the
cold, wild iridescence of the
far north, whitening the
curtains of mist that hang
over the rocks farther up the
fiord-like inlet or *voe*, as it
is called, and accentuating
the black verticals of the
derelict jetty, like the ribs of
a drowned Viking ship.
And while it is not true to
say that the June sun never
sets in this northern
archipelago, there is no
midnight darkness, nothing
more than a twilight
expressively known in the
islands as 'summer dim'.
Stepping stones to Norway
and to the snow-covered
lava of Iceland, the Shetlands
were vitally involved in the
Viking invasions of Scotland,
Ireland and England. Norse
blood runs in the veins of the
people and comes out in
their language. Like Orkney
the islands were under
Norse dominion until 1469.
    The beached boat calls
attention to the Shetlander's
dependence on the sea. That,
until the discovery of off-
shore oil, with its already
manifest power of trans-
forming the traditional life
of the islands, was his chief
source of livelihood, apart
from the famous industries
of the Shetlands, the making
of garments from the
distinctive wool of the native
sheep and the breeding of
ponies.

Trevelgue Head, Cornwall
The photograph speaks of
the remoteness and romance
of Cornwall; it also illumi-
nates the relationship of
sea and granite cliff. The headland slopes towards the
water and it is clear that, as
Victorian geologists
observed, the upper part is
receding more rapidly than
the base, so the effects of
wave and storm, so
impressive, so powerfully
stirring to the imagination
and so eloquently present
even on this midsummer day
in the form of the dead,
contorted tree, contribute
less both to erosion and the
shape of the cliffs than rain
and land springs.

There seems to be nothing
in this landscape which is
alien to the natural scene,
and yet the cliffs owe their
character in part to the
activities of man. For more
than eight centuries, from
the early Iron Age and
during part of the Roman
period, men lived and
worked on these inhospitable
headlands. They built a
promontory fort, one of the
best surviving examples of
the type common in
Cornwall, and left traces of
their stone-walled huts and
of their occupation –
metal-working. The remains
of iron mines have been
found under the cliffs, as
well as of rock-cut furnaces.
Nearby two round barrows
joined by a bank of earth
stand conspicuously on the
edge of the crag. Excavation
revealed crouched skeletons,
one of them clasping a
polished battle axe.

with oyster catchers and a variety of seaweeds. King Arthur's Castle, as it is
called, though it has nothing to do with that folk hero, being, in fact, a Norman
castle and Celtic monastery, stands on its fierce headland. It looks down into
the harbour of Boscastle and over the long beaches of The Strangles with its
jagged rocks, where many sailing ships have been wrecked. High Cliff, at the
south end of the beach is the highest in Cornwall at 708 feet. The path leads on
to Cambeak and Crackington Haven, where the shore is a litter of curious grey
and white stones, right into Widemouth Bay. Finally the path ends at the border
of Cornwall and Devon, at Marshland Mouth, a lonely, rocky beach, typical of
all Cornish beaches, with a little stream running into it through sloe bushes and
honeysuckle.

The river Taw flows through Barnstaple and out to the three-mile stretch of
Saunton Sands. Along the coast Ilfracombe, Lynton and Watchet take you on
into the Bristol Channel, to the Severn Bridge across into South Wales, and west
to Pembrokeshire, where the coastline and seascape is similar to that of Cornwall. But before you cross into Wales it is well worth climbing Selworthy
Beacon, 1,014 feet high, just west of Porlock, to enjoy the wonderful views over
the Bristol Channel into Wales, and over Exmoor, into Devon.

This flat land running west from Chepstow ends at Cardiff, with its huge docks,
its population of 300,000, and its city spreading along the banks of the river
Taff. Here the Bristol Channel is held against the lush meadows of Monmouthshire by a twenty-four-mile-long sea wall.

This is now an industrial landscape again. Beneath steeply wooded hills the
steel works of Port Talbot and the city of Swansea lie between the gritty sand
of Sully Bay and the majestic cliffs of the Gower Peninsula, past The Mumbles to
Worms Head, overlooking the golden sands of Rhossili Bay. Worms Head is
one of a number of nature reserves stretching back along the coast to Porteynon.

On one side of Carmarthen Bay the sands of Pembrey, some six miles long,
are backed by pine forests and dunes; on the other are the famous Pendine
Sands, one of the longest, firmest, flattest stretches of sand in Britain, which were
used for attacks on the world car speed record. Just off Tenby is Caldey Island.
Further on are the bird-haunted islands of Skomer and Skokholm with their
buzzards and ravens, and most westerly of all is St David's Head and Ramsey
Island.

The coast now begins to be backed by mountains all the way from St David's
Head to the Cheshire Plain, with Anglesey standing off across the Menai Strait,
overlooked by Caernarvon Castle. In the distance, over the saltings, is the
eternal presence of Snowdon. It is a far cry from the gentle beaches of the east
and south coasts. Through the Menai Strait and past the castle at Beaumaris is
Puffin Island, where these colourful birds breed on the rocky, grass-topped cliffs.

The industrial centres of the Wirral Peninsula, Ellesmere Port and Birken-
head, and the holiday town of New Brighton, cluster together on the river
Mersey and fade gradually into Morecambe Bay, where the landscape is almost
more 'advanced', with the nuclear power station at Heysham and the oil

refinery and chemical works near Middleton. This coast, with its sand and shingle beaches, is famous not only for the shrimps of Morecambe but for the flat fish and salmon in the estuary of the river Lune.

The rivers of the Lake District, like the Duddon, Wordsworth's favourite river, come down into Morecambe Bay, where the cries of birds mingle with the noise of the sea. All along this Cumberland coast the grass cliffs are of boulder clay right up to the Solway Firth and the wooded hills falling to the rocky cliffs and tidal saltings of the river Esk.

A landscape of islands emerges on the rocky, indented coastline of Scotland – the coast of Inverness, Ross and Cromarty and Sutherland. The wild Isle of Rhum, with its crags and bleak moorland, is exposed on its west coast to the full fury of the Atlantic. On Eigg there are 'singing' sands, caused, it is said, by grains of quartz being rubbed together. The fishermen and crofters who inhabit Canna, a green, fertile island, are reputed to enjoy an earlier spring than elsewhere in the Hebrides. The tall, red basalt peaks of Skye fall to boulder-strewn beaches, perhaps one of the most romantic spots on the whole long coastline, with its purple heather, its whitewashed crofts, and the farmlands and woods in the north-west and south-west.

What better place to end a journey round the coasts of Britain than Cape Wrath, the most northerly point of the Western Highlands, a headland tall and barren, dominated by the cliffs of Clo Mór rising sheer for 900 feet three miles to the south-east.

Flora and Fauna

This long coastline is the home of a large variety of birds, insects, flowers and seaweeds. Not all shores will support life, of course, other than the miniscule flies and insects that live amongst some seaweeds. On shingle beaches and on sandy foreshores you will find the yellow horned poppy, sea campion, sea bindweed and sea beet. Sand couch grass and marram grass flourish on sand dunes, helping to consolidate the shifting sand, and hold in place the lovely plants of sea holly and sea rocket. Here and on salt marshes these plants grow alongside the blue and yellow sea aster, the pink sea milkwort, that odd whip-like plant eel-grass, and samphire.

On sandy shores are found those 'curiosities' of beaches, the egg cases of certain fish, clusters of common whelk eggs, eggs of the shellfish *Purpura,* from which purple dye once was made, cuttlefish, the empty shucks of dogfish, often called 'mermaid purses', and the black purses of skate's eggs, which have a pair of horns at each end.

When you come to the rocky shores of Cornwall and Pembrokeshire, which are warmed by the Gulf Stream, and higher up the coast by the North Atlantic Drift, the cliffs in spring are miniature gardens covered with blue squills, sea pink or thrift, sea-lavender, scurvy grass, the white stonecrop, the biting yellow stonecrop, and Scots lovage.

Top St Brides Bay, Pembrokeshire
The photograph prolongs a moment of pure magic. The sun has just been swallowed by the sea, only one little family still lingers on the much frequented beach. The tortuous, fantastic folds in the magnificent headlands and the Pre-Cambrian rocks they embrace are brought into one dusky harmony in the failing light. The island of Skomer (named by the Vikings who harried this coast for centuries during the age of the native Welsh princes) lies like a basking whale on the horizon. The island is the scene of one of the largest concentrations in Britain of three penguin-like birds – the puffin, the guillemot and the razorbill – and there too, many of them nesting in rabbit burrows, lives a colony of shearwaters.

Bottom Nigg Bay, Cromarty Firth, Easter Ross
The green corn of June waves from the foreground of the picture to the dark trees at the water's edge, enhancing the tranquil mood of the northern evening landscape when all the wild irregularities of crag and boulder and ravine are smoothed by distance and the westering light into rounded shapes of clearest mauve and purple. The low mountains on the far side of Cromarty Firth, among them Ben Wyvis, rise abruptly from woodland and more rich farmland. The contrast between stretches of arable country and rough, untillable steeps is characteristic of Ross.

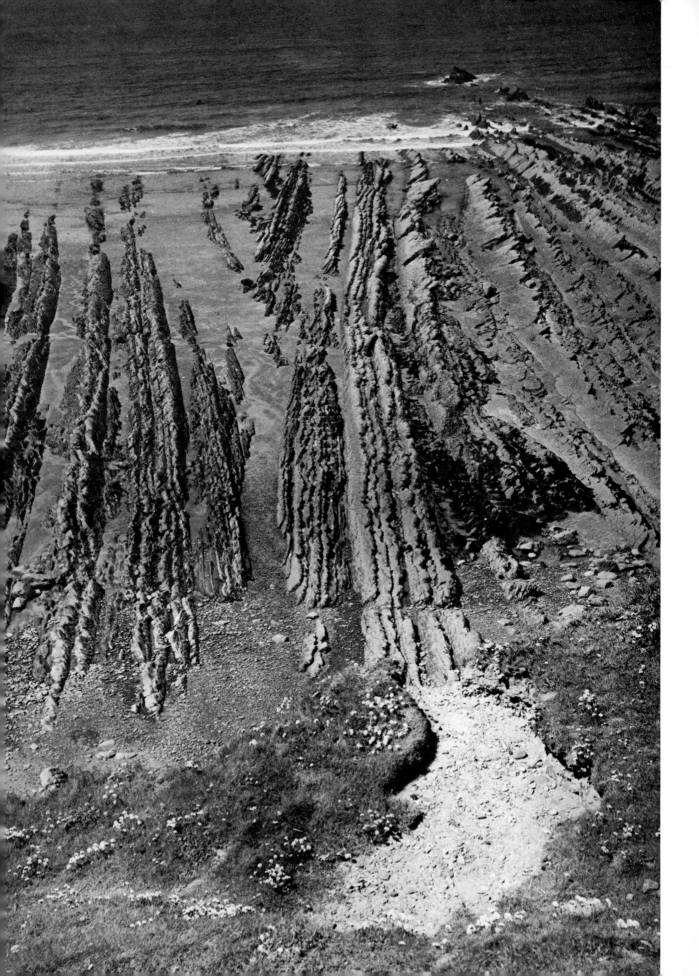

The shore itself is the habitat of many types of seaweed, from the channelled wrack lying above the tide-mark, to the red seaweeds which thrive in deep pools lower down the beach. Channelled wrack is grooved along one side of its fronds to prevent it drying up as the tide recedes. Lower down still there are various other wracks – flat, bladder and knotted. Bladder wrack supports some 40,000 creatures to the square yard. Some of these are, of course, minute and only keep alive on the moisture provided by the seaweed. Nearer still to the sea is the serrated wrack, which has no air bladders. It is a greenish brown compared with the deep brown of other seaweeds.

Oarweed grows in lower shore pools, a large plant with a stem that widens into a strap and then divides into fingers. Here, too, can be found tangle weed, sometimes as long as twelve inches and resembling a large ribbon crimped at the edges, bootlace seaweed and, lastly, red seaweed, the colour of which comes out in fresh water. Women used to dry these red seaweeds to make rouge and other cosmetics.

In amongst the seaweeds millions of shells litter the sand. Dull when the tide is out and the sand dry, they are polished and alive with brilliant colours when the sea washes over them again. Delicate reds, pinks, whites, browns and magentas adorn the sand, with mauves, violets and orange. These shells are the remains of such creatures as limpets and mussels, or piddocks, which, when alive, are phosphorescent at night, giving out a pale bluish-white light.

Then there are the razor shells and the prettiest of all shore shells, the cowries, which, when they are living, have red tentacles speckled with yellow. The shells were once used as a form of money in India, China, Arabia and Africa. The auger shell, a beautiful narrow spire named after the boring tool, the top shell, cone-shaped and glossy, and the Venus shell lined inside with delicate shades of every colour, can be found on most sandy beaches.

The rock pools are the homes of all manner of small fish, from the grey gurnard and the reddish sapphirine with its blue fins, to the bullhead and the cobbler. One of the most interesting small fish is the butterfish or blenny. On the east coast they are known as nine eyes because they have nine white-edged black spots each side of the dorsal fin. The pipe fish lives exclusively on plankton, the microscopic drifting organic life that provides food for marine creatures.

On sandy beaches crabs abound, especially the hermit crab, the cuckoo of the shore. It has no shell of its own and has to steal from other creatures, generally from the whelk, which first it eats before moving into its new home. The smallest of all crabs is the pea crab, which makes its home under stones. Along with them live barnacles and anemones, those blobs of jelly left stranded when the tide recedes. Yet when the sea covers them again their colours light up – pink, yellow, white and pinkish brown. For all their delightful names – beadlet, strawberry, daisy, dahlia and snake locks – these are flesh-eating creatures which poison their prey before swallowing it up. Oddly enough one of the most beautiful shore creatures is the seaslug, three inches long, greyish white and not unlike a tiny shaggy sheep. It lives on anemones, but is unaffected

Welcombe Gap, Devon Charles Kingsley wrote an apt description of the coves of North Devon: 'to landward all richness, softness and peace; to seaward a waste and howling wilderness of rock and roller, barren to fisherman and hopeless to the shipwrecked mariner'. The passage precisely conveys the aspect of Welcombe Gap. We look down on these strangely parallel and sinister reefs of cruel, jagged shark's teeth rocks from a cliff speckled with thrift and trefoil, while behind us furze bushes give way to a luxuriant valley of meadows and oak trees watered by a crystal, fast-running stream. The tooth-image is reinforced by the local reference to such coves as 'mouths', and these ferocious jaws recall those of the monstrous Dinichthys of the Devonian Age when the dark muds were laid down which provided the glistening shale of the black corrugations and the slaty sand between them. The striking linear formation at right angles to the cliff is due to the action of the sea, which has hollowed the beds of rock between the shales.

Staffa, Inner Hebrides
The name of the island is Norse and means Stave Island, for the black basalt columns of which the whole sea-girt rock is composed are reminiscent of the upright timbers of which the Norsemen built their stave churches. This extraordinary geological formation was the result of repeated and violent volcanic eruption during the Tertiary era and it was because the lava consisted mainly of basalt, which has the tendency when cooling to take the shape of six-sided columns, that Staffa assumed its arresting and formidable aspect. The gigantic upheavals followed a line across to the Giant's Causeway, and the rock formations are identical.

by their stinging tentacles, incorporating, in some way, their poison as an extra protection against its enemies. The more anemones it eats the more poisonous its back becomes.

Sea birds feed on many of these shore creatures. In winter the four main types of gull – the common, the herring, the blackheaded and the black-backed – congregate at the tide line, where they can often be seen dancing on moist sand close to the waves. They do this to bring worms to the surface. These birds are scavengers and have pale eyes and cruel beaks.

On rocky cliffs the kittiwake makes its nest of seaweed lined with grass. One of the most graceful of sea birds, the tern, or sea swallow, goes south in winter, but the little tern, the sandwich and the common tern nest here on grassy banks or sand dunes, where they lay their brown-spotted, stone-coloured eggs. On the approach of danger huge crowds of these birds rise from the cliff and float out over the sea. It is a most dramatic sight.

The gannet is a diving bird and more powerful than a gull. From a height of 200 or 300 feet a gannet will dive after herrings or other shoal-swimming fish. They congregate in gannetaries off the north of Scotland, near the Firth of Forth, on the Bass Rock and at Grassholm off the Pembrokeshire coast.

The largest birds to be seen from the shore are the cormorant and the shag. They also dive for their food, but not with quite the beauty and *élan* of the gannet, the greatest diver of them all. These three birds are of the pelican family; they nest together on rocky islands off the coast, and their short, harsh croaks fill the air.

The puffin makes his nest in a burrow in the grass, or in a hole in the cliff; the razorbill is a sturdy flier and sometimes migrates as far as southern France. The guillemot, and the black guillemot, which is seen only in northern seas, nest on open ledges of the cliffs.

Some of the most beautiful sea birds are the waders, which can be seen at the edges of the shore. The loveliest of all is the oyster catcher, black and white, like a magpie, with a reddish-brown bill and slightly paler legs. As they skim over the surface of the sea, they utter their cry, 'pink-a-pink-a-pink'. The turn-stone is seen mostly in winter, searching for food beneath the pebbles, as its name implies.

Sandpipers and redshanks also frequent the shore, while the lapwing is mostly found beside estuaries and mudflats. Probably the smallest shore bird is the rock pipit. It is the only perching bird which likes the beaches, exploring seaweeds after the tide has gone down, and filling the air in spring with the sound of its sweet trilling song.

Off the west coasts, from the Shetlands to the Scillies, are to be seen the shearwaters, the Manx, the great and the sooty. This last arrives from New Zealand in summer. They get their name from their sloping, banking movement, flying like aircraft, with stiff wings, both high and low over the water.

The fulmer, which is greatly increasing in numbers in the south-west, is a curious bird. It lays only one egg and to protect it disgorges an oily substance, in the same way as an octopus will eject a black inky fluid. In the old days, on St Kilda, where they nest in large colonies, the people used to kill them for food and extract the oil for their lamps.

The Cornish chough is now, alas, seen no more in Cornwall, where it was once so numerous that it was adopted as the county crest. I know of only one, an old male, who returns annually to the cliffs near Newquay. The chough is a member of the crow family but of slenderer build, with its black plumage, bright red legs and a red, curved beak. Although they still breed prolifically in Wales, in Cornwall they have surrendered to their enemies – the jackdaw and the farmer, who believed them to be vermin which killed sheep. All attempts to reinstate the bird in Cornwall have so far failed.

9 Moors and Heaths

Moors

THE chief characteristics of moorland are space, wide open views and immense birdswept skies. Lapwings, skylarks and dunlins nest here, while kestrels and merlins can be seen on the northern and western moors, hovering in wait for their prey. In summer the prevailing colour of moorland is the purple of heather; in winter, if the moors are not covered in snow, the colour is the grey of the predominant granite or the brown of dead bracken.

Tors or hills stand out on the moors in a landscape which is treeless and uncultivated, its shallow soil lacking in lime. On lower ground a layer of peat will cover the bleak expanse, but in spring and summer the moorland is coloured by vast swags of gorse above the heather.

Moors, like mountains, are one of the permanencies of landscape, and have been called the 'last wildernesses'. This is true even of the small moor in Wigtownshire, to the north-west of Newton Stewart and south of the Carrick. To reach it from Dumfries, the road passes through thick pine forests, which hide the moorland behind the reservoir of Clatteringshaws Loch.

South of this wild and beautiful road is a fertile farming landscape, with creameries at Dalbeattie, and salmon fishing in the river Cree, which runs through Newton-Stewart. After you have passed through the town, the road forms a square about this moorland, with Mochrum Castle and its lake to the south, Colmonell to the north and so back by the A714 to Newton Stewart.

Within this square is a landscape of grey hills and windswept moorland with few houses. In May and June the moor is covered with heather and the white downy heads of cotton grass, which flourishes in the boggy soil. The outcrops of volcanic granite, which may be seen in the houses of Dalbeattie and Creetown, are a delicate silvery colour against the purple heather.

Grouse are protected birds on this moor, dependent on the heather for food and cover. In autumn the heather is burnt to encourage new growth for the birds. All four species of grouse live in Scotland, each inhabiting a different landscape. The red grouse lives in the heather-bearing moorlands; the black prefers the grass clearings of woodland; the capercailzie lives in coniferous woodland; and the ptarmigan, an Arctic tundra bird which changes the colour of its plumage, from speckled grey in summer to pure white with black tail tips in winter, exists only on high bare mountains.

The Roman Road, Blackstone Edge, Yorkshire No legacy of the occupation so forcefully expresses the implacable Roman attitude to subject lands and people as their road system. This was the chief means by which the conquerors imposed a coherent unity on the motley of populations under their dominion. A glance at the Ordnance Survey map of Roman Britain shows how relentless was the progress of the Imperial roads, how they cut across all the rich variety of the countryside without regard for its physical idiosyncrasies, enmeshing the land in a controlling web as rigid as that of the Victorian railways and the motor highways of our own day. The sense of iron control persists even in Roman roads no longer in use, such as this ghostly stretch of the remarkable road that ran from Littleborough in Lancashire to near Ilkley in Yorkshire. It is 16 ft wide with kerbs and ditches on either side. Where the road mounts steeply, the central paving stones are deeply grooved, possibly to accommodate the brake-pole on vehicles descending the declivity.

Opposite Fylingdales Moor, Yorkshire
The flawless geometry of the great white spheres, each echoing the shape of the white sun and reflecting every change in the light of the cloudy morning, sharpens the sense of personal insignificance in this grand, treeless expanse.

Below Goldsborough Pasture near Brunswick Bay, Yorkshire
The high Yorkshire moors, a Jurassic sandstone plateau, reach right to the sea on their east side and Goldsborough Pasture, with its medieval ridge and furrow pattern of open arable fields, is swept by salty breezes.

The north-eastern moorlands of Yorkshire cover 1,000 square miles and lie to the east of the A1, which follows more or less, the route by which the Roman legions travelled to Hadrian's Wall. Here is Egton High Moor overlooking the river Esk, which is noted for its salmon; Goathland Moor, with its mile-long section of Roman road, crossing Wheeldale and Pickering Moor. Here the North Yorkshire Moors Steam Railway connects Pickering to Grosmont, near Whitby.

Further east is the famous Fylingdales Moor, where the empty moorland behind Robin Hood's Bay is dominated by the radomes of the Air Ministry Ballistic Missile Warning Station. Nikolaus Pevsner describes these huge ping-pong-like white balls as 'the geometry of the space age at its more alluring and most frightening'.

Helmsley Moor, with its vast fields of heather and, here and there, a few pine trees, shelters one of the glories of Yorkshire, Rievaulx Abbey in the Rye valley. The splendour of this Cistercian monastery is the ruined presbytery and choir of seven bays with stone-ribbed vaults and beautifully moulded capitals and corbels below the triforium, which is carved with foliage. Dorothy Words-worth notes in her *Journals*, in the entry for 15 July 1802, how she came to

View from the Churchyard
of St Mary's, Whitby,
Yorkshire
The cross high above the
town confronting the setting
sun and the moors beyond
the Esk reminds us of the
great date in the early
history of Whitby, the Synod
of 664 which resolved the
differences between the
Celtic and Roman churches
by accepting the Roman
system. The scene of the
photograph is famous for the
working of jet (fossilized
conifer), one of the oldest
industries of our land. It
flourished during the Bronze
Age and throughout the
Roman occupation and in
the Middle Ages and was
revived with outstanding
success in the 19th century.

Rievaulx from Thirsk: 'Arrived very hungry at Rivaux. Nothing to eat at the
Millers, as we expected, but at an exquisitely neat farmhouse we got some
boiled milk and bread; this strengthened us, and I went to look at the Ruins.
Thrushes were singing, cattle feeding among the green-brown hillocks about
the Ruins. These hillocks were scattered over with *grovelets* of wild roses and
other shrubs, and covered with wild flowers. I could have stayed in this solemn
quiet spot till evening, without a thought of moving.'

Rievaulx, as seen from the long curving terrace overlooking the ruins, has
changed very little today. Nor was Dorothy Wordsworth the only artist who
admired the Abbey ruins: Turner painted the scene, and the poet Cowper, too,
wished 'to stay forever'.

One of the most exhilarating sweeps of moorland can be seen from the road
which runs from Middleton in Teesdale to Alston. To the left, five miles out of
Middleton, is High Force, England's highest waterfall. Here the river Tees,
turning round the sharp face of the steep Cronkley Scar, falls seventy feet over
a black cliff of the Great Whin Sill, into a deep pool below, enclosed by shrubs.

Now the road sweeps excitingly forward to a wide expanse of fell and moorland, past Langdon Common, Yad Moss and Alston Moor. In winter this is a
high, cold country, with snow drifts over fourteen feet deep at times, almost
cutting off the whitewashed farmhouses and the few cottages grouped together

in a huddle of stunted trees. Even High Force freezes in really hard winters. Sheep and grouse are the chief 'inhabitants' of these moors; cattle find pasture in the more enclosed places. From Alston, reputed to be the highest market-town in England, it is but a short car-ride to the wilder border country crossed by Hadrian's Wall.

Probably the best-known moors of the West Riding are Keighly and Wadsworth because of their nearness to Haworth, where the Brontë sisters lived. Haworth itself, with its cobbled street, the Parsonage and the church, is a tender memorial to the whole Brontë family.

A lane near the Parsonage leads out to the moorland, where in the cold winter weather of December 1848 Charlotte went to search for a sprig of heather, thinking it might revive her dying sister Emily. Today Haworth is a dark town of mills and cottages set in hard and sombre moorlands, sometimes lifted up against a leaden sky, their margins flowing together. This autumn the hawthorn hedges along the roads were covered in giant convolvulus with harebells growing below. In winter these moors will become interfolding acres of white and blue.

The dry-stone walling, grey in sunshine and black under rain, is a miracle of design and craftsmanship. The walls on Rylstone Fell flow over the moors, dividing the grassy hills.

On Masham Moor dark clouds hang over Wensleydale, where grouse shooting is about to take place. From the higher parts one can look across these acres of heather to the sun shining in 'sweet' Nidderdale, to Great Haw, 1,786 feet, and Great Whernside, 2,310. Under such dark cloud the moors turn a deep green beneath the stillness of heather and gorse. Here and there this expanse is

Haworth Moor, Yorkshire
Here again, as in other photographs of the Yorkshire moors and fells, the brilliant light reveals traces of much older field systems, particularly to the left of the picture, where wall and hedge follow the line of what was probably once the boundary of an early Saxon estate. Yet it is not the record of its geological and historical past that makes this wide, windswept landscape significant and moving, but the knowledge that it was this scene which nurtured the extraordinary genius of the Brontës. Here in this wild sky and harsh *chiaroscuro* the principle of storm is manifest which animates the mystical unique vision of Emily.

broken by a reservoir, such as that at Leighton, where the brown terraces stand beyond the park-like landscape below the moors of Kirkby Malzeard. Late at night you seem to be moving across the top of the world, through ever-increasing folds of darkness and silence.

In this silence the elegant, black-and-white-legged Swaledale sheep roam the moors, their small heads adorned with curved horns. They are the intimate inhabitants of these last pockets of landscape between the industrial towns of Burnley, Halifax, Bradford and Leeds.

Dartmoor is an area of granite tors and sweeping moorland, wooded valleys, ancient stone circles and peat-coloured streams. The boggy part of the moor, to the north, is the source of most of Devon's rivers. The average elevation of the Moor is 1,200 feet; the highest tors being Willhays and Yes Tor. Heather covers the upper slopes, giving way to rough grazing below, but over the centuries wind and rain have denuded the high rocks of any soil at all. The streams that criss-cross the moor create acres of bog, very green and very dangerous. It is unwise to leave the roads without a guide, though you can safely enter the many Forestry Commission woods which are scattered all over the moorland.

Enormous vistas of loneliness spread out before the walker or rider on this moor, from Cranmere Pool in the north, to Lydford Gorge in the west,

Butterton Hill to the south, and the ancient neolithic Grimspound, not far from Chagford in the east, where Conan Doyle laid the scene of his novel, *The Hound of the Baskervilles.*

When you leave the sloping lane and go into the circle at Grimspound, or visit the forty hut-circles on Standon Hill, above Tavy Cleave, where the river comes down over massive boulders, or stand beneath Bowerman's Nose, an immense block of granite south of Haytor, you feel that you have slipped back in time. This feeling is prevalent both on Dartmoor and on Bodmin Moor to the west in Cornwall.

Stand on Combestone Tor and look across the wild landscape, with hardly a house to be seen, to Sharp Tor, Sherril and Corndon. The colouring is gentle, from the sunlit brown of the granite, through the bright brown of autumn bracken, to the deep green meadows in front of the almost black conifer forests and the blue of distant tors. Go down to Fingle Bridge near Moretonhampstead, where the river Teign rushes through deep woodland, and walk along the Fisherman's Path, and you will hardly know that you are in moorland

View from near Grimspound, Dartmoor, Devon
The dramatic granite rock in the foreground is a characteristic Dartmoor tor which may have formed a stack when the sea, which covered Devon and Cornwall in the Pliocene period, smoothed the surrounding land. The whole landscape is remarkable for the great number of hut circles (more than 1,350) which make the prehistoric scene a living reality. Grimspound, near to the scene of the photograph, is a walled Bronze Age village.

country. But come back to the granite outcrops above the deep gorge at Lustleigh Cleave, and you feel not only the great age of Dartmoor, but its present ability to lift the mind and soul above the everyday.

A large number of heathland plants grow about the moor – heather or ling, bell heather, tormentil, Cornish moneywort and marsh pennywort, lichens and liverworts. Gorse is almost as common as heather, and everywhere there are ferns and mosses with their descriptive names, like the alpine hair moss, urn-fruited hair moss, pale dwarf bog moss, cavern moss and rusty swan-necked moss.

At times the wilderness blooms with bog pimpernel, bogbean and the little bog orchid, with whortleberries, which grow on certain parts of the moors and appear to fruit even on barren rocks. Regal-looking cattle and black-faced sheep roam the moor fields, while foxes run in the deep coombs, and ponies, the lineal descendants of the Anglo-Saxon 'wild horses', gallop and prance in the meadows beyond the dry-stone walls. The air of the moor is filled with their whinnying, and the lonely sound of sheep bleating. In the heart of the moor, buzzards fly over that strange group of trees, Wistman's Wood.

To go down Lydford Gorge is to descend into a fairyland of wild flowers, water, deep-green ferns and brown stones. The descent is steep. Tall trees almost roof in the slippery steps, but once over the bridge at the bottom, you are in a mile-long landscape of rapids and cascades, the banks carpeted with bluebells and wild garlic. This is a green 'lost' world where birds flash in the sunlight between canopies of leaves. The beginning of the Gorge, where the river Ock falls to the valley, is echoed at the further end by a splendid waterfall, the clear white water falling into the peat-brown of the stream below.

The moorland is split by the waters of rivers: the West Dart, the Okement, the Avon which rises at Rider's Hill and flows southwards into the sea at Bigbury Bay, and by the still waters of reservoirs such as Burrator, below Sheepstor. These moorland rivers are crossed by sturdy, dependable bridges, such as that at Postbridge, or at Dartmeet, or by the ancient clapper bridge at Two Bridges, where kingfishers are often to be seen, or where the river Bovey tears down its valley to the Becka Falls.

Such waters flow beneath the high tors, which form doors into the secret inner wards of the moor. Saddle Tor, for example, is a group of rocks in the shape of a saddle, where everything is deserted and lonely, and where cloud comes down suddenly to envelop the entire moorland. The mist may descend quickly, too, over that ancient stone circle, the Grey Wethers, a mysterious megalithic monument, of which there are more than ninety on Dartmoor. They symbolize, in the landscape, the immense age of the moor.

To get above the cloud and the mist one should climb the high hill at Brentor, not far from Lydford Gorge, in that corner of the moor just north-east of Tavistock. From the small church at the top you can see not only large sections of Dartmoor and the sea in Whitesand Bay, but northwards to the tors of Bodmin Moor in Cornwall. If the weather is fine, a whole map of landscape is laid out below you.

Tin mine near Tavistock, Dartmoor, Devon
The relics of a dead industry impart an air of infinite melancholy and romance to the wide landscape. Ores of tin found their way into the cracks and veins of the granite masses of Dartmoor during gigantic volcanic earth movements. Copper as well as tin was mined in this part of Dartmoor. Both were prehistoric industries and both flourished in the Middle Ages. There was another boom in the early 18th century which lasted throughout the middle decades of the Victorian period. Traces of the earlier activities scarcely exist. The landscape in front of us, with its overgrown, desolate spoil heaps and roofless, windowless ruins and tall, pointing chimney stacks, is a 19th-century creation.

Opposite China clay spoil heaps near St Austell, Cornwall
Clay, like tin, derives from the Cornish granite and these gleaming pyramids are the waste of the thriving St Austell china clay industry.

Below 'Brown Willy', Bodmin Moor, Cornwall
The name is a corruption of the Celtic *Bryn Huel*, the tin-mine ridge. Like the rock in the photograph of Dartmoor (page 177), 'Brown Willy' is a granite tor. The two summit outcrops are the ruins of an Iron Age fort.

The tors of Bodmin Moor – Rough Tor, Brown Willy, Garrow and Kilmar Tors in the centre of Twelve Men's Moor, to name but a few – reflect the hard granite cliffs of the sea-coast. Here streams of brown peaty water run down to the low meadows and create bogs. The streams are crossed by clapper bridges leading to lost tracks, which once were used by traders from Wales and by smugglers from the north-coast harbours of Boscastle or Port Isaac, or the lonely shores of any navigable beach, from Bude to Padstow.

In the disused granite quarry near St Breward, above the De Lank river, gardens of wild flowers grow in the stone walls above small pools of green rain-water. Far out over the moor, from Garrow Tor, overlooking the river, there are deserted, ruined homesteads of what were once tiny agricultural holdings. You can still see the granite walls which hedged in their gardens, and come suddenly upon a gnarled apple tree in blossom, or an old rose blooming in the shelter of a stone wall. Now sheep creep into such places for 'homing' against winter winds and snow, and foxes use what remains of old neolithic huts below Rough Tor for shelter. Ponies huddle together in the warmth of the Forestry

Commission's wedges of conifers, or come down to water to the new reservoir on Crowdy Marsh, or to Siblyback to the east.

In spring and summer butterflies frequent the walks through the conifer forests, and sheep and ponies use these avenues to cross this section of moorland, oblivious to the A30 cutting Bodmin Moor in half on its way from Launceston to Bodmin Town, with the high tors on the right, and Dozmary Pool on the left. It was here, according to Tennyson, that Sir Bedivere threw King Arthur's sword, Excalibur, when the King himself lay dying in the sedge. Above the pool and further to the east is that long moorland group of wind-swept rocks, the Cheese Wring, above its quarry at Minions. The village here was once the site of an early industrial development, but all is now dead and gone, and only the traces of the mines are left.

To the south-west of the moors this landscape is honeycombed underground by disused mines – lead, tin, copper and arsenic. Above ground ruined engine-houses and their chimneys stand out like ruined cathedrals in the loneliness of the moor below Caradon Hill. Yet the stonechats, chaffinches and linnets never stop singing from the gorse bushes lining the deserted railway tracks leading to the quarries. Above kestrels and buzzards hover in the open moorland skies searching for prey.

These birds are the essential inhabitants of these wild landscapes. The common buzzard frequents these moors, with its dark-brown plumage, its pale underside marked with bars and streaks, its broad wings with its slotted tips, and its rounded tail. The buzzard's main food is rabbit, and when myxamatosis ravaged the rabbit population they became scarce; now that the disease has waned, buzzards have returned in appreciable numbers. One of their characteristics is an exceptionally keen sight, their eyes reputedly being eight times sharper than human eyes in spotting details.

The southern landscape of Cornwall is dominated by the china clay mines and their 'slag' heaps on Gossmoor, near the town of St Austell. Now that clay mining has extended into Bodmin Moor, the white spoil heaps are beginning to override Rough Tor itself. China clay is a decomposed form of elvan, a substance not unlike granite. The manufacture of English porcelain owes its beginnings to William Cookworthy, who set up a factory in Plymouth in the eighteenth century. But however necessary these clay mines may be to the economy of Cornwall, the spoil heaps, both at St Austell and on Bodmin Moor, have completely changed the landscape, if not ruined it. Their whiteness is a scar on the land.

Bodmin Moor, although the largest moorland area in Cornwall, is not the only one. The moors about Camborne in the centre of the county are scattered with the ruins of tin mines, this being the most productive area. About Zennor, behind Penzance, are the moors of West Penwith. In this lonely landscape one is always in reach and sound of the sea breaking on the shore below Gurnard's Head. On these upthrusts of granite moorland, brilliant in the light from the sea, are neolithic forts, villages of prehistoric tin-miners as well as ruined nineteenth-century mines, of which the engine-houses at Botallack are the most

impressive. These barren uplands are the haunts of sea birds as well as buzzards and kestrels.

Surpassing all other natural phenomena, to my mind, is the flight of the great starling flocks in late autumn. In vast black groups these birds sweep in suddenly from the coast, twisting and turning like fast-moving storm clouds, and pour away down some gap in the moorland hills, travelling at great speed until they reach their night's roosting-place in the woods of North Hill on the east side of the moor. Whatever the explanation of these flights, and the precision with which they are carried out, there is no more wonderful dusk-time sight when November is already icing over the moorland grass, and the berries of the spindle tree in the stone hedges have turned to pink and are ready to drop.

The 265 square miles of the Exmoor National Park lie mostly in west Somerset, extending over the boundary into north Devon. Exmoor is more intimate,

Exmoor, Devon
Although the countryside of Exmoor, curlew-haunted and grazed by small distinctive hill sheep, imparts as deep a sense of antiquity as Dartmoor, it is visually very different, primitive indeed, but pastoral. It began to take its present shape 250 million years ago during the Armorican earth folding. Exmoor is formed of sandstone supporting heather moors worn into deep coombes which prehistoric man found too densely forested for settlement.

gentler, more 'beautiful' than other moorland. It does not, as do the remote fastnesses of Dartmoor and Bodmin Moor, or the Yorkshire moors, seem to repel you as if you were a stranger and unwelcome.

The high points of Exmoor are Selworthy Beacon and Dunkery, from which there are fine views over the entire moorland. There are fine walks over Gods-end Moor to Withypool, below Worth Hill, which give one a closer understanding of this 'cultivated' moorland scenery.

It is not far, along the river Barle, to the Tarr Steps, a medieval packhorse bridge over the river, the finest clapper bridge in the West Country. It is an exciting place when the river is running high under the fifteen great clappers, huge blue one-piece granite slabs, resting on buttressed piers of granite blocks. The river is wide here; the valley deep and wooded. You can feel the 'climate' of Exmoor in the valley of the Barle, the rounded heather hills, the deep blue of the water and the green woods above it. Blackmore set his novel *Lorna Doone* in this romantic landscape. Through a window in the tiny church at Oare, Carver Doone shot Lorna.

With luck, on this moorland, it might be possible to see a Montagu's harrier, a bird which lives on lowland heaths and in young conifer plantations. The male is grey with a black wing-bar and is, of course, a bird of prey. In April wrens, chaffinches, willow warblers and a cuckoo or two are singing in every copse beside the streams, the banks of which are luxuriant with wild leek, campion, and in certain places fine specimens of royal fern.

Heaths

Heaths are tracts of lowlands found mainly in East Anglia, in Hampshire, in east Devon, and the Lizard Peninsula in Cornwall, where alone is found the Cornish heather. The other most prolific heathland plant is gorse, which often supports the parasitic flower, dodder. Heathlands, because of the nectar in heather, are the haunt of bees. Apiarists often carry their hives up to a nearby heath at the time of the honey flow.

Breckland in Norfolk, at one time one of the finest heaths in the country, changed with the coming of the Forestry Commission plantings and the 'Battle Area' west of East Wretham. Yet this sandy region, once called the East Anglian Desert, can still excite. For all the massive new pine forests, this land is so ancient that you feel it might not be impossible to come upon some lost tribe existing here with primitive arts and rituals.

This sandy region is, also, a region of flint. Houses, cottages and pubs are built (or, at least, faced) with black flint, as the Brandon variety is known to distinguish it from Norwich flint. Not far from Brandon itself, in a clearing in the forest, is Grime's Graves. The flint miners of 2000 BC walked here where you walk, came to these dark pits, and went down into them by means of leather ladders, until they came to the bed of floor-stone. This was the type of flint they used to make their agricultural and hunting tools and weapons.

At the bottom of these pits lead off tunnels, along which neolithic man burrowed. You have to go down on your hands and knees to get into them, while above your head a mild wind is blowing in the millions of trees. The sound reaches you below, like the noise of the sea heard from a distance.

Breckland, nevertheless, preserves, here and there, its original farming amongst a flora of heather, ling, gorse and bracken, with fields of rye and sugar-beet about the flint farmhouses and the foresters' cottages. Over all there is an exquisitely sharp, enlivening air, softened by the waters of the Little Ouse, into which the river Thet flows by Thetford, once the cathedral city of East Anglia, and lit by the beauty of cinnabar moths, the nervous movements of wheatears, and the wonder of the bee orchid.

A bird sometimes heard in heathland is the nightjar. I have often heard and seen it in East Anglia, for it nested near a mill-house I rented. That other heathland bird, the Dartford warbler, is only found in the south. The commonest butterflies are the green hairstreak, the silver-studded blue and the grayling.

Thomas Hardy, writing of the Dorset heathland which he called Egdon in *The Return of the Native*, describes all heaths: 'The great inviolate place had an ancient permanence which the sea cannot claim. Who can say of any particular sea that it is old? Distilled by the sun, kneaded by the moon, it is renewed in a year, in a day, or in an hour. The sea changed, the fields changed, the rivers, the villages and the people changed, yet Egdon remained.'

Corfe Castle, Middlebere Heath, Dorset
This exquisitely composed landscape, solemn, mysteriously lit, brooding and romantic, is exactly that painted by Paul Nash and at the same time it evokes the spirit of Hardy's noble tragedies, which appealed so strongly to the painter.

In the Domesday Book the heath is called *Bruaria*, a wilderness of briers. The ruins, magnificently set on their Purbeck hill occupy a unique place in history. The castle was begun very soon after the Conquest in 1086, to protect Poole harbour. After being successfully held by the Royalists under Lady Bankes in 1643, the castle was betrayed to the Roundheads and blown up by order of Parliament.

10 Bridges and Modern Roads

Bridges

Two of man's finest achievements in landscape are roads and bridges. Roads have only reached the status of architecture in the last half century; bridges, always an architectural delight, have now become feats of engineering.

The transition from architecture to engineering began with the first cast-iron bridge over the river Severn at Coalbrookdale, an arch of 100-foot span, built in 1779 by Abraham Darby. Cast iron later gave way to steel and reinforced concrete, which today can be seen so effectively used in conjunction with the new motorways.

In total landscape many older bridges have become (as the great modern bridges have yet to do) moulded into the scenery as much as the houses beside them and the streams or rivers which they cross. The clapper bridges, for example, described in the last chapter, are some of the oldest, most efficient bridges of their time. Based on the principle of the oldest bridge of all, the tree trunk thrown across a stream, a clapper bridge is built of flat-topped boulders placed at regular intervals in the water, on which are laid flat stone slabs six feet wide.

Examples are to be seen at the Tarr Steps on Dartmoor. At Postbridge the clapper bridge which once carried the road from Plymouth to Moreton-hampstead has been restored to give a complete picture of a pack-horse crossing. One can generally recognize a pack-horse bridge, since it is too narrow for a cart but wide enough for a horse carrying panniers. When you stand on the lawn-field looking at it, you see beyond it another development, the bridge built in the trees to carry the eighteenth-century road.

In medieval times bridges sprang up all over the country. The fourteenth-century bridge at Bradford on Avon in Wiltshire looks chunky and solid with its nine arches, its white stone slightly greened with age, its parapet a straight line beneath the houses of the town and the woods beyond. The bridge across the river Dee at Llangollen, known as one of the Seven Wonders of Wales, also dates from the fourteenth century. An even more interesting example is the thirteenth-century triangular bridge at Crowland in Lincolnshire. It looks grotesque, out of place, and leading nowhere in the streets of the town, until you realize that these streets were once streams. Halfway up the wide stone steps of the bridgeway is a 200-year-old figure of Our Lord holding the World in His arms.

The Iron Bridge, Coalbrook-dale, Shropshire
This light lacy bridge, arching in two concentric semicircles over the Severn, has something of Adam elegance which is set off by the foreground rushes and the half rural aspect of the farther river bank. And yet the structure might stand as a symbol of the whole modern industrial landscape. For Abraham Darby built it to serve his Coalbrookdale iron works which in the 1760s he had expanded to become the largest factory of any kind in the kingdom. It marked the beginning of the creation of industrial England. The Iron Bridge, cast in 1778–9, was the earliest bridge of cold cast iron. Darby's works occupied and ravished a romantically beautiful valley, chosen because the iron ore was close at hand in the carboniferous rocks. Despite the destruction of natural charm, Arthur Young found something heroic in the industrialized landscape of Coalbrookdale: 'The noise of the forges, mills, etc., with all their vast machinery, the flames bursting from the furnaces with the burning of the coal and the smoak of the lime kilns, are altogether sublime.'

Opposite top Clapper bridge above Dolgellau, Merioneth This bridge could be ascribed as convincingly to prehistory as to the present.

Left Folly packhorse bridge, Llanfrothen, Merioneth, built of local slab and granite by Clough Williams Ellis.

Above Packhorse bridge, Glen Lyon, Perthshire Bridges of this as of the clapper type are ageless so it may be true that the

Romans built this crossing over the Lyon during their campaigns against the Picts almost 2,000 years ago.

Right The Town Bridge,
Bradford on Avon, Wiltshire
In the green hilly landscape
embracing Bradford on
Avon the bridge plays a key
part as a link between the
two tiers of buildings on
either side of the river,
joining them with nine arches
of the same local yellow
limestone of which they
themselves are fashioned.
Though originally constructed in the 13th century, the
date of two of its arches,
the bridge is thoroughly
17th-century in character,
dominated as it is by the
unmistakably Jacobean
central feature with its
ridged dome and pinnacle.
This was once a medieval
chapel, but after the bridge
was rebuilt it was known as
the Blind House or Lockup,
to which purpose it
continued to be put until
the present century.

Opposite The Triangular
Bridge, Crowland,
Lincolnshire
Few places bring us into
sharper contact with the
medieval scene than this
stone hump left high and dry
by the receding waters of the
Welland. In the 14th century
the river divided at this
point into two streams, often
flooded, and the tripod-
shaped structure was
designed to span them both.
According to the medieval
chronicle of the nearby
abbey, the *Historia
Croylandensis*, there was
a bridge of exactly the same
shape as early as 943. The
mysterious weatherbeaten
crowned figure of Christ
seated against the ancient
wall above the rough uneven
paving is thought to have
filled the gable of the abbey
church before it was taken
down in 1720.

Most of the ancient bridges are enormously sturdy. The thirteenth-century
Monnow bridge over the Wye at Monmouth has a military tower at one end
and a gate where custom money was collected. The twelfth-century bridge over
the river Wear at Durham, Elvet Bridge, is complete with its own chapel, built
by Bishop Pudsey.

The chunky sturdiness has given way to the lightness and delicacy of the
modern bridges of steel and concrete. The development was, however, through
such glorious stone bridges as that across the Thames at Richmond. Designed
by James Paine and built in 1774, it is, perhaps, the most famous of all classical
Georgian bridges in England.

From these elegant bridges a new age emerged with such colossal examples
as the Forth Bridge in Scotland. The two main spans of this cantilever bridge,

Above Richmond Bridge,
Surrey
The balustraded bridge, with
its rhythmic crescendo of
arches, was built in 1774–7
by James Paine.

Opposite top The Forth
Bridge; *bottom* The New
Forth Bridge, Midlothian
The glassy water emphasizes
the massive strength of the
original Forth Bridge of 1890
built on the cantilever
principle.
   Beside the swelling and
contracting rhythms, the
colossal girders and
ponderous strides of the
Victorian achievement, the
New Forth Bridge (1958–64)
looks plainly horizontal and
incredibly light.

which was opened on 4 March 1890, are 1,700 feet each, and the whole length
is over a mile. Another development is the steel arch of the Newcastle upon
Tyne bridge, built between 1925 and 1928. It carries what was then the Great
North Road, now the A1, across the river Tyne.

Such bridges lead inevitably to the new colossi: the Severn road bridge, the
Tamar bridge, and that now under construction, the Humber bridge. Two
concrete legs of this bridge are already to be seen high above the north bank of
the Humber. When completed it will span the river from Hessle, a suburb of
Hull, to Barton-Upon-Humber in Lincolnshire. It will be the longest single span
bridge in the world, 367 feet longer than the Verrazano Narrows bridge in New
York, which is 4,359 feet long.

The beauty of these new bridges, which dominate their landscapes, lies in
their economy of construction. They seem to float over the rivers, over the
motorways, dividing the countryside with elegant white arcs.

There is no more lovely sight than the Severn bridge with the sun setting
behind it, the concrete roadway now turned to pink, held up by an immense
bow of wire slung from its terminal piers high in the sky of approaching night.
The vertical wires hold the roadway to the bow like a colossal harp. The bridge

The Severn Suspension Bridge, Aust, Gloucestershire
No one will deny that this mighty structure of 1966 has a certain elegance. But a comparison of the crude shapes of the steel pylons with the stone piers of Brunel's Clifton Bridge, or even with the rudimentarily traceried piers of the New Forth Bridge, brings out the want of ornament and the distinction between a work of art and a work of engineering. This bridge is nonetheless a tremendous work of engineering, 3,240 ft long with pylons 400 ft high.

has all the sophistication of modern technology, and an aerial beauty as if it were itself in flight.

These modern colossi exist beside older bridges. Beside the new Tamar road bridge, for example, is that masterpiece, the railway bridge built by Isambard Brunel. It was completed in 1859, the year he died, and still carries the Great Western Railway, as it was then called, from Devon to Cornwall over the river Tamar. The central pier, built in a huge cylinder, went down eighty feet below the water before it reached bed-rock. Then, by means of jacks, the sausage-like trusses were raised so that piers could be built under them. This delicate operation was watched by vast crowds, and the work was conducted by Brunel himself from a platform on the truss.

It was, of course, Brunel who in 1864 built that superb suspension bridge at Clifton, spanning the Avon Gorge some 245 feet above the water, and so joining Gloucestershire to Somerset. The most beautiful parts of this bridge are the twin towers at each end, high above the woods both sides of the Gorge, as elegant as the town of Clifton itself.

Yet despite these modern wonders, these mighty feats of engineering, one returns to the intimate pleasure of the country bridges. To Smeaton's bridge at Perth, for example, its lovely pink arches and blue iron parapet, built between 1766 and 1771 over the river Tay. Because the Tay often floods here, the foundations were made inside coffer dams. Smeaton himself, of course, is better known for the Eddystone Lighthouse off Plymouth; each stone section was made in Wadebridge, Cornwall and ferried out to the rock.

That lovely turnpike bridge, Lockleys old bridge, two miles north of Welwyn Garden City, is no longer used. Now it forms a splendid green walk over the stream, its red brick contrasting with the forest beyond. When it was built in 1834, it carried the Hertford road from Welwyn; when the road was altered, the bridge and the turnpike lodge became marooned in the countryside.

And there are many other lovely bridges: the little bridge over the river Coln, opposite the Swan Hotel at Bibury in Gloucestershire; the elegant, single-span bridge over the river Kennet at Newbury in Berkshire; the Shaking bridge over the river Conway at Llanrwst, with the mountains behind it; Greta bridge in the North Riding, which John Sell Cotman painted; Eckington bridge over the

The Clifton Suspension Bridge, Bristol
This is a powerful instance of the enhancement of nature by a man-made addition. The graceful, airy bridge suspended high above the Avon emphasizes the drama and grandeur of the river passage through the deep gorge. And although the structure is a work of engineering by an engineer, Isambard Kingdom Brunel knew how to combine engineering with art. The heavy limestone pylons are superbly architectural.

river Avon in Worcestershire; or that greystone bridge over the blue water of the West Dart at Hexworthy on Dartmoor; or any of the old, secret bridges down forgotten lanes, over forgotten streams all over the country.

Modern Roads

Four modern developments have radically altered our view of traditional landscape. The first is the aeroplane, which allows us to see landscape as a map; the second is television, which in programmes about the countryside selects landscapes to bring into the home; the third is the motorway. Whereas the first two do not alter the landscape, the third does, because roads slice through it. The fourth, our speed of travel in landscape, alters it most of all, whether it be along old roads or new. Speed forces us to view a landscape into which we are going, rather than viewing the landscape in which we are actually at rest.

Modern landscape architecture is very different from the 'architecture' practised by 'Capability' Brown, for example, or Humphrey Repton. Today the architect of modern roads must plan vast forward spaces ahead, from a base which is never static. Brown placed a tree, or a group of trees, beyond a lake which, like the mock temples and follies, were to be viewed from behind windows or from appropriately placed terraces. If the viewer strayed from the house, the landscape was approached slowly, on foot or on horseback.

Today, with the speeds attained on motorways and other trunk roads, the planning has to be done fifty miles ahead, because we are no sooner into one landscape than we are out of it. We travel down endless concrete channels. The film, as it were, has gone before we have taken it in; we need to have the screen at least ten miles in front of us to appreciate the smallest detail of landscape.

The effect of this is, of course, to diminish the landscape we see from the new roads. Only the broadest effects can make an impression. What I will call 'smudge' landscaping is all that matters – great wedges of colour, green in spring, red in autumn, defined lines of bare twigs and branches in winter. Only these can destroy the appalling monotony of these hundred-mile-an-hour roads.

The effect of this 'moving' landscape can be seen clearly on a television screen, particularly in the case of a race course. It is fascinating to watch the background of landscape beyond the cameras focused on the racing horses. The smudge landscape, which appears to be moving with them, is exactly the same as that created by a car moving at speed up a motorway. It is a 'travel' landscape. The woods, trees, and farm buildings pass into the long line of fir trees as if you were in a dream, the white rails of the course moving too. The distant trees are flat and unleaved; the smudge landscape unrolls in a kind of snow scene, though it is spring and under sunlight. As soon as the horses begin to run, you are jolted out of the static landscape of weeds and grass by the starting-cage, until you are once more brought back to reality when the race ends, a reality of solid landscape of green paddock, unsaddling enclosure and the coloured vests of the jockeys, or the railway lines, the parked cars and the rows of new houses.

This is an Alice-in-Wonderland landscape, very similar to the motorway experience and as disturbing, since in neither case is it possible to fix oneself firmly into the landscape. In short, both television and motorway turns the countryside we know into a fluid landscape, to which we must adjust. We are unable to hear the noises of landscape. We are cut off, in our cars, from the music of the countryside to such a degree that we are no longer of the world we inhabit. With the new motorways we are out of our depth, we have left the comfort, the excitement, the refreshment of the old landscapes. However beautiful the new roads, we are still lost and made neurotic by their speed.

But they do have a peculiar beauty of their own, an heroic beauty, a frightening Valhalla-ish beauty which is gone as soon as we observe it. We rush into the scenery ahead which we can no longer touch. And touching the 'furniture' of landscape, is, perhaps, the most important of all. This sense of touch establishes the all-important relationship between ourselves and the landscape. It cannot be achieved at such modern roadscapes as Spaghetti Junction, where the modern motorways interrupt the ages-old landscape. Until they can settle into a landscape of their own, they will remain alien and remote. They have to learn from the old roads.

One of the virtues of these established roads is that, between the stone wall or natural hedge and the road itself, there is usually waste ground. Where poisoning of such waste ground has been stopped, large numbers of plants will grow. They are of vital importance to ecological health and to the inhabitants of landscape, and so to us who use and delight in landscape.

The wide verges of motorways should be left rough to grow nettles, cranesbill, forget-me-not and soapwort – never mind what they look like. The walls separating the verges from the meadows should be ivy-covered, and wild briar and blackberries encouraged to grow as they grow down most of the lanes which are left. No doubt much of this is being done, but since there is no stopping on such new roads, it will be necessary, in order that one may appreciate the 'travelling' landscape, to seed mile upon mile with wild flowers.

Perhaps we should not despair. Perhaps there are future possibilities on such major roads, for the standard of road design is improving encouragingly. Trees are being planted and new routes are being planned to harmonize with contours and land forms to disturb our countryside as little as possible.

Index